# The
# Good Cat
# Spell Book

# The
# Good Cat
# Spell Book

## GILLIAN KEMP

**CROSSING PRESS**
Berkeley | Toronto

To the Fleet Street journalists John Evans and Jack Pleasant
who inspired me to begin writing. To you the reader, to
all cat lovers, and to my father, who is allergic to cats.

Crossing Press
an imprint of Ten Speed Press
PO Box 7123
Berkeley, California 94707
www.tenspeed.com

Distributed in Australia by Simon and Schuster Australia, in Canada
by Ten Speed Press Canada, in New Zealand by Southern Publishers
Group, in South Africa by Real Books, and in the United Kingdom and
Europe by Publishers Group UK.

Cover and text design by Chloe Rawlins

Library of Congress Cataloging-in-Publication Data
Kemp, Gillian.
  The good cat spell book / Gillian Kemp.
    p. cm.
  Includes index.
  ISBN-13: 978-1-58091-188-7
  ISBN-10: 1-58091-188-9
  1. Cats—Miscellanea. 2. Magic. I. Title.

  BF1623.A55K46 2008
  133.4'4—dc22

2008020467

Printed in China

First printing, 2008

1 2 3 4 5 6 7 8 9 10 — 12 11 10 09 08

# Contents

# CHAPTER 1

# The Cat as Your Familiar

Cats are believed to possess the power to bewitch people. But people can bewitch cats, too. Call "Puss Puss" or "Kitty Kitty" to a cat and more often than not, he will approach you.

The magic has already begun if a cat has wandered into your life and adopted you as his owner. That cat has already bewitched you, and it is your duty to respect, look after, and love him.

A familiar is an animal companion who helps his person in their magical work. Your cat is your familiar because the pair of you loves each other. You know your cat loves you when he follows you around the house, insists on sleeping on your bed, and shadows your every move. Your cat identifies your different tones of voice and responds to you with unique meows, purrs, and mannerisms. The love you and your cat share is a psychic and magical bond that creates profound loving power that enhances your magic and increases the potency of your spells. The stronger the love link between you and your cat, the stronger your spells will be. As your familiar, bound to you by enduring love, your cat delivers your wishes. You and your cat's patience and respect for each other will release and channel magic.

Your cat must trust you and feel safe and secure in your love. Love is the connection to the spiritual realm. The spiritual realm is where your spells are activated because this is where you connect to the light of the universe and the source of all life. The bond of love cannot be broken—not even by death.

Naturally possessing intuitive insight, your cat probably knows and understands you better than any human. If your cat is your familiar, you will create an interdependence with him in which neither of you is complete without the other because your lives are inextricably intertwined. Cats of either sex symbolize the abundant, maternal essence we call upon for help.

Cats' eyes represent the clairvoyant eyes of inner intuition through which we see the truth to discover ourselves and our place in the world. If you look into their eyes you will see the true, clear sight of omniscience, the seed of divine all-knowing. Look into your cat's eyes and you will have a window into the psychic world.

Cats see in the dark what a human cannot. Bast, the cat-headed goddess who presided over ancient Egyptian temples, represented the threshold of enlightenment where the conscious and unconscious minds met and blended. Whether you believe in spells or not, you can invoke the powers of Bast to help protect your familiar from harm and to bring your cat a long and happy, healthy life in your care.

Magic is your inner power to direct events. Focusing your thoughts on what you want and wish and hope for is what brings results. The more people who direct their thoughts toward the same wish, the more powerful the spell—because their minds are channeled in the same direction. It is the same when you are working with your cat. He can add natural potency to your spells because of the emotional and psychic connections you share. Your faith in your spell also has an impact on its efficacy. Belief brings positive results in spellcasting.

Facing east when spellcasting gives extra vitality and power, because the sun rises in the east. If you have a garden where your cat has a favorite place to relax and where you feel good, you can connect more directly with the elements and life-force energies. Every part of nature, including animals, trees, plants, and the weather, is an occult link to wish fulfillment. Spells for love, happiness, wealth, and health enlist the forces of nature.

Light is the energy of God and the universe. Nothing in nature can live without it. Light is also warmth, which is essential for life. When you light a candle, you link into heaven's will and blessing by evoking the power of light. The thought or spoken words you put into lighting the candle continue to ascend to the heavenly or higher light for as long as the candle continues to burn. It is the same with incense.

Your cat will help you in a variety of ways to do your magical work, offering guidance as well as magical tools. For thousands of years, their actions have been interpreted as omens and the things they have discarded from their own bodies have been used for magic. For some spells, you'll need whiskers, milk teeth, fur, and claws that your cat has shed. Store them in a small "cat magic" trinket box until you require them for sorcery.

Your familiar may be trying to tell you something through his behaviour, giving you cues you can follow to enhance your magic. For instance, cats love digging their claws into carpeting and furniture for fun. When they do this, wish for something that you would like to have within your grasp. They also like the best seat in the house in the warmest spot, so wish for something or someone to warm toward you when your familiar takes your chair. And when your familiar sits on your lap, listen tele-pathically to what he is saying to you. Paying attention to your cat will develop your intuition and psychic abilities.

When you extend your finger to your cat and he clings to it with his velvety paws, wish for something or someone you want to cling to you. Silently, your cat may be telling you to grasp a situation and hold on to someone or something coming your way.

When your cat is lazing in a sunbeam, he may be trying to get your attention to tell you something or someone sunny is about to enter your life, to bring light and happiness to you. Wish it if you want it. And when your cat's eyes shine like lanterns, your familiar may be telling you that you are blessed by heaven or that something good is about to happen for you. Ask for the light in your cat's eyes to shine on you and for the eternal light of love in your soul to keep burning brightly.

Your cat is your friend for life, sharing your working hours and soli-tary moments. Your familiar seems to know weekdays from weekends, too. Cats appear to have a built-in clock that makes them lick your face, nuzzle you with their nose, or walk around your head with small butting, touching, and leaning gestures a little before the alarm clock is set to go off. They know a lot about relaxation, comfort, and sleep. Cats are peace-ful to have around.

When you cast your spells, do not be put off if your cat gives you one of his snooty looks as if to say, "I don't think much of you, you must be mad," and starts licking his paws and washing his face. Connect to your cat's behaviour; your cat speaks without words. Allow your familiar to guide you on his magical path, and let him work his age-old cat magic on you.

# CHAPTER 2

# Cats as Objects of Worship & Fear

Cats gained their magical reputation for many reasons in different eras. They are creatures of the night, their meow is unearthly, and they love to sleep all day. Their pupils alter from a narrow vertical line by day to a luminous globe like the full moon at night. A cat luckily dupes fate by always landing on her feet. Her eyes follow things she appears to see that are invisible to us. Cats also seem to turn up from nowhere, take to us, and adopt us as their keeper. They have a mystery all their own.

The word *cat* occurs in numerous different languages, but "Puss" is derived from the name Pashtaor Bast, the cat-headed Goddess Bastet worshipped by the Egyptians thousands of years ago. Egyptian figures and paintings of the period show cats wearing earrings and jeweled collars, and thousands of mummified cats have been found in tombs and buried along the Nile. So revered were cats in ancient Egypt that family members would shave off their eyebrows as a respectful sign of mourning and as sympathetic magic when their cat died. Killing a cat was a crime that carried the death sentence.

It may have been that every home had a cat for the simple reason that cats kept out mice. A home without a cat was not "homely." The cat was found in the centre of Bubastis, in the centre of Rome, and in the centre of the family, guarding the hearth. The original domestication of cats is lost in antiquity. But it is believed the cat originally made her way from Libya into Egypt.

The ancient Egyptians regarded the cat as the "flaming eye of the sun," Lady of Life, the soul of Osiris, and the eye of Ra, the sun god. The Egyptians believed that when the sun sank below the horizon every night, cosmic combat took place between Ra, the god of light, and Apep, the serpent of darkness. The cat was symbolic of the creative powers of the sun, which rose every morning, having destroyed Apep. But Apep, being immortal, reappeared every night. And so the Cat's Cradle, a string game, was invented as sympathetic magic to control the movements of the sun on which their lives depended. The game is still played today by children worldwide.

Bast, the goddess worshipped by the ancient Egyptians, sometimes had the complete body of a cat, but sometimes the head of a cat and body of a human dressed in embroidered garments. At the height of her power Bast was revered as patroness of the eastern part of Nile delta, in the region called Tell-Basta, in Bubastis. An amulet found there bears a message that reads, "May Bastet give life and power." The cat was thought to be a symbol of eternity and immortality because of the way it curls its tail around its head to form a circle. It was also believed to have nine lives, thanks to its agility and tenacity. The number nine has long been believed to be lucky because it is a trinity of trinites. In Egyptian astronomy there were nine spheres, and the Egyptian pantheon had nine gods. Nine was also significant to the Greeks: Apollo—brother of the moon goddess, Artemis—created a nine-month lunar year. And in Christianity it is believed that Jesus died at the ninth hour.

The Egyptians and the Greeks associated the cat with the moon as well as the sun. Bast's parents were moon deities, and her son Khensu was a moon god. Her father was Horus the sky god. Demetrios Phalarios, a Greek poet, wrote that the size of a cat's body increased as the moon grew from new to full and decreased as the moon waned. Sometimes the cat's eyes changing from crescent to round were likened to lunar phases. "They shine more fully at the full and more dimly in the changing and wane," wrote seventeenth-century bestiary author Edward Topsell. A cat's behaviour, often becoming more active after sunset, is associated with the moon.

The cat cult of ancient Egypt continued well into the Roman period. The Romans called the cat *cattus*, the origin of our word "cautious." After the demise of cat worship in Egypt, similar practices sprang up in India, China, and Japan, and "cat clans" emerged in Teutonic, Celtic, and other lands. Pictures of Freya, the Norse goddess, show her chariot drawn by two cats.

By medieval times, cats were feared instead of worshipped. Cats' nocturnal instincts, intelligence, luminous eyes, and unearthly cries, and the static electricity of their fur earned them the reputation of possessing demonic powers, and so cats suffered persecution, along with the people who owned or befriended cats.

An epidemic of witchcraft persecution raged in the fifteenth, sixteenth, and seventeenth centuries in Europe. Witches were believed to be in sympathy with the devil, whom they supposedly met at nighttime *sabbats* to concoct mischief and devilment. To attend a sabbat, it was believed, a witch would anoint her feet and shoulders with the fat of a murdered baby, then mount a broomstick, and exit the household chimney into the nighttime sky.

From 1450 to 1750, no men, women, or children, including nuns and monks, were safe from being accused of witchcraft. Not attending church was a sign, and talking to your cat was another. Many people were condemned as witches simply because they kept household cats.

Witchcraft paranoia arrived in Britain in 1563 and even spread to Salem, in the Massachusetts colony, in 1692. Two women were executed for witchcraft in Northampton, England, as late as 1705.

Jane Wenham, the last person to be tried for witchcraft in Britain in 1712, was accused and found guilty at the Hertford Assizes of "conversing familiarly with the devil in the form of a cat." But she was pardoned and lived until 1730.

Many witches were convicted for sending a "wantounne cat" to avenge people. They were also accused of having "carriers," cats who stole milk, cream, cheese, and meat to be feasted on at sabbats. A black cat being called a witch's "familiar" originates from a medieval superstition that the devil's favorite form to take was that of a black cat. At the beginning of the fourteenth century, when Pope Clement V overthrew the Knights Templars, some tortured members of the order confessed to worshipping the devil in the form of a black tomcat.

In England, however, the white cat was considered unlucky because white made her visible to her prey. But since white cats often have one eye a different color from the other, they have always been considered to be magical and more capable than any other cat to predict good fortune. If your familiar is a white cat, it is believed you will have exceedingly good fortune your whole life long. Within twelve months after you acquire your white cat, someone in your close family will marry.

A deaf white cat with blue eyes is said to be especially psychic because her impeded hearing is directed inward to her inner ear, psychic centre. And blue-eyed cats of any color are said to be especially magical because, like blue sky over nighttime darkness, they symbolize divine eternity and immortality.

Folk beliefs about cats have persisted into modern times. In England in the nineteenth century, sailors' wives liked to have a black cat as a pet. They were well fed on fish, in the belief that the black cat could and would charm safety into the lives of the women's husbands at sea. For further good luck, some wives sent their husbands off to sea with a little black fur cut from the cat's coat. In the fishing communities it was considered lucky if a black cat ran toward a fisherman, and a sign of a bad catch if the cat crossed the fisherman's path to his ship or boat. Because black cats were considered lucky, they were frequently stolen.

The spells in the following chapters draw on cat wisdom that has survived the test of time. All are offered in the spirit of doing good, never doing harm.

# Lucky Cats

According to age-old tradition, it is a lucky sign when a black cat crosses your path: "When you are walking along the street it is a lucky sign a black cat to meet."

- It is lucky to be visited by a black cat and unlucky to shoo a black cat away.

- To dream of a black cat is a premonition of good luck, happy news, or a delightful event.

- To possess a black cat who grows one white hair is a sign of luck in love and affairs of the heart.

- If you see a black cat, stroke it three times and make a wish. Your wish will come true.

- Buddhists believe that light-coloured cats ensure a wealth of silver and that dark-coloured cats ensure a wealth of gold.

- If a tabby or gray wanders into your home, it is an omen of money.

- To own a tortoiseshell cat is a sign that you will always be lucky.

- It is a lucky omen if a cat wanders into your home and adopts you.

- Cats with double claws are thought to bring luck to their owners.

- A cat acquired in the month of May is said to be a cat more likely to catch birds and snakes than rodents.

# CHAPTER 3

# Spells for Love & Romance

$L$ove is everybody's favourite feeling, including your cat's. Your cat is a strong love-link who carries the wisdom of the nature of the higher world because he lives in the etheric—that is, in a subtle form of energy on a higher plane than matter. It is in the ether that the elements of air, fire, water, and earth are put into action and take effect to become matter. The ether comes from the origin of the universe, which is love.

Your cat has supernatural ability to see the unseen, and by harmonising with his love frequency, you connect through him to the love wave in the ether so that it runs through you and carries you along to where you want to be. The love frequency flows through every living part of nature. By aligning yourself to the supernatural forces, you can direct love to you because the supernatural forces are ruled by love and are sympathetic to your inner resonance.

Friday, ruled by the love planet Venus, is the most potent day of the week for casting love spells. In general, it is best to perform spells to bring love to you while the moon is waxing (becoming full) and spells to drive unrequited love away while the moon is waning.

# TO BEWITCH THE ONE YOU LOVE

*This is a good springtime spell to perform when love is in the air and your feline friend is molting and feeling frisky. You will need:*

- Fur from your cat's brush
- Clean white paper
- A pen or pencil
- One pink candle
- One blue candle
- A saucer
- Milk or water

Brush your cat or stroke his fur. Remove the fur from the brush or your fingers, and place it on an unused piece of white paper.

With your cat present, light the pink candle to represent yourself and a blue candle to represent the one you love.

Write your name on a small piece of white paper and the name of the one you desire beneath yours. Sprinkle cat fur over your names, and fold the paper into a small envelope shape to contain the fur. Burn the paper in both flames while saying,

> *As fur burns in this flame,*
> *Into your mind enters my name.*
> *As your name burns,*
> *To me your heart turns.*
> *During my cat's nocturnal hours,*
> *[name of cat] will work on you his magical powers.*
> *I will be in your dreams while you rest,*
> *Until you grant my love request.*

Place the paper in the saucer to reduce it to ashes and play with your cat while the candles burn. Tell him you know he will help you to win the heart of the one you desire. Snuff the candles out. Bury the ash. Wash the saucer and pour some milk or water into it for your cat to drink.

# TO DRAW ROMANCE TO YOU

*You will need:*

- A lavender-scented incense
- One pink-coloured or rose-scented candle
- A little cat fur

Light the candle and the lavender incense, and make sure that both are safe. Switch off all electric lighting, and lie down with your cat's heart across your heart. Stroke your cat until he purrs. Breathe in rhythm to the purring to link to the slow alpha brain waves that connect you to the ether where all knowledge is.

Tell your cat that you are asking, with your cat's help, for the light of the candle flame to bring a perfect partner into your life. Then say,

*Cat be nimble,*
*Cat be quick.*
*As the flame burns the wick,*
*Bring me true love quick.*

If when your cat is on your heart and you are stroking him, you see or feel static electricity, it reveals that you have created a magic spark of attraction, perhaps in the life of someone whom you have already met. Do not try to create static, but take it as a good sign if it occurs naturally.

After relaxing as long as you like with your cat, sprinkle a little of the fur that may already be on your hands, or picked up from your clothes, into the candle flame. Then snuff out the candle.

# TO ATTRACT A NEW LOVER

*Friday night would be the most potent time to cast this love spell. You will need:*

- One pink or red candle
- Rose oil
- A straight pin

Stroke your cat with your fingertips and anoint the candle with rose oil, from the top to the centre, to attract love toward you and your cat.

Using the pin, write on the candle the name of the one you desire. As you light the candle say,

*This flame of love will ignite flames of passion that burn within the heart of [name of person]. She [or he] will love me.*

At midnight snuff out the candle saying,

*My wish is sealed by the witching hour.*

Take your cat to bed with you to seal the spell. Wait in the patience of time, and the one you have bewitched will contact you. Alternatively, your paths will cross as if by coincidence.

*You will have a male visitor if your cat washes his face with his right paw over his right ear. If he washes his face and left ear with his left paw, expect a female visitor.*

# TO KEEP THE ONE YOU LOVE

*The new moon is the best time for this spell. You will need:*

- A cat brush
- One silver candle
- A handkerchief or scrap of cloth
- Red cotton thread
- A needle

Settle your cat beside you and light the silver candle at the time of a new moon. Brush your cat's fur and remove the fur from the brush. On a handkerchief or scrap of material, use red cotton to stitch the first name and surname of the one you desire in running stitch, inserting strands of fur to secure them by the thread as you stitch.

Sleep with the handkerchief under your pillow, and the one you love will be true to you. If you decide you want to walk away from the relationship, undo the stitching and burn or bury the handkerchief, thread, and fur.

# TO ENCOURAGE A LOVER'S
# FEELINGS TO GROW

*You can make love grow if you start this spell at the new moon. Catmint (Nepeta faassenii) is governed by the love planet, Venus. You will need:*

- A garden, or potting compost and an indoor pot
- A catmint plant

Dig a hole in your garden, or place some potting compost in an indoor pot and push a catmint plant into the soil. Ask your cat to make paw prints in the soil. As the catmint grows, so too will love for you grow in the heart of the one you desire.

# TO ENCOURAGE A LONG-TIME
# LOVE TO ENDURE

*Start this spell when the moon is waxing. As a symbol of the soul and life, salt can be used as a charm to perpetuate a relationship. You will need:*

- An unused envelope
- Salt
- One pink candle

During the waxing phase of the moon, drop a pinch of salt into an envelope and place it in or beneath your cat's bed so that he will sleep on it.

When the moon is full, light a pink candle and slowly sprinkle the salt into the candle flame. As the flame burns blue, say,

> *When the Moon is round*
> *Good luck will abound.*
> *Seek and you shall find,*
> *What is now within your mind.*
> *Your thoughts shall always turn to me,*
> *You and I will always be we.*

Snuff out the candle. Roll the envelope into a ball shape and roll it across the floor so that your cat chases it, the way the one you love will chase you.

# TO ATTRACT YOUR SOUL MATE

*When measuring your cat's shadow, make sure the sunlight is behind you so that the shadow is in front. Your will need:*

- A long ruler or measuring tape
- Lipstick
- A pen with green ink
- A piece of red, pink, or green paper

When your cat is stretching, perhaps to sharpen his claws, or curled up basking in sunlight, measure his shadow from nose to tail.

Put lipstick on your cat's right front paw. To take your cat's paw print, encourage him to step onto the small piece of pink, red, or green paper, or stand him on the coloured paper, or press the piece of coloured paper, to his paw. Write beside the paw print the length of the shadow. Fold the paper to conceal the paw print and the number.

Put the piece of paper inside your right shoe. When you go outside, say in your mind to the rhythm of your walk,

*I will attract my soul mate,*
*And be asked for a date.*
*Like cat love I wear in my shoe,*
*True love come to me to woo.*

You will find that you will attract a partner. When you do, be discerning and question yourself about whether the person is right for you.

# TO PERSUADE AN UNWANTED SUITOR TO RETREAT

*Do this spell during a waning moon. You will need:*

- An unused envelope
- Salt
- Access to a running stream or river, or to the sea

Place an unused envelope containing three pinches of salt in your cat's basket, under his bed, or wherever he will happily sleep on the sealed envelope for a few nights. By being in close contact, the salt will be influenced by your cat's feelings.

Take the envelope of salt to a running stream or a river, or to the sea when the tide is going out. Throw a pinch of salt into the water, saying,

*[Name of person] the tide has turned.*

Throw in a second pinch, saying,

*You will flow out of my life.*

Throw in a third pinch, saying,

*I have broken from you in my mind.*

Sprinkle the remaining fragments of salt into the water and bury the envelope. Walk away without looking back, to leave the past behind you. The person concerned will painlessly flow out of your life, as surely as streams flow to rivers and rivers flow to seas.

# TO ENCOURAGE AN UNWANTED
# LOVER TO LET GO

*You will need:*

- One blue candle
- Two straight pins

Leave a blue candle in your cat's basket during a waxing moon. The feline powers he exudes will be absorbed by the candle.

When the moon becomes full, insert a pin through the candle from left to right so that it pierces the wick and appears through the wax on the opposite side. Cross the first pin as closely as possible with a second pin pressed through the wick from left to right. The pins should cross paths.

With your cat purring beside you, light the candle. Ring the bell on his collar, if he has one, to clear the air and to draw down power from heaven to earth.

As the candle burns through the pins, the lover you are redirecting will realise that the relationship is over. If the pins move around while the candle is burning, turn the candle around to point the pin tips in the direction of your lover's home. The person will get the point and withdraw. The crossed pins provide a crossroads so the person can find other directions to take. Snuff out the candle after it has burned past the pins.

# TO END A RELATIONSHIP

*This type of spell is known as a banishing and is most effective when performed during the waning moon. You will need:*

- Milk or water
- A pen with black ink
- Clean white paper
- One white candle

Pour enough milk or water into your cat's dish so that he drinks but leaves some. Write the name of your lover whom you wish to leave you in peace on an unused piece of white paper. Beneath the name write,

*Realize I do not want a relationship with you.*

Draw a thick black border around the words. Flick milk or water from your cat's bowl onto the paper. Leave the paper to dry.

With your cat settled and purring beside you, light a candle and burn the paper in its flame while saying,

*By candle light and cat bright eyes,*
*Feline purrs chase vermin good-byes.*

The person on whom you have cast your spell will sense that you have detached yourself in your mind. The effect the spell will have is that this person will either suddenly contact you to see whether he or she still has power over you, or withdraw without resistance.

# FOR A LOVER TO RETURN TO YOU

*You will need:*

- One red candle
- One pink candle
- A ballpoint pen
- Two bay leaves
- A little fur from your cat's brush
- Two paper clips
- An unused envelope or one that your lover has written your name upon

Stroke your cat with both of the candles so that your cat's personality and personal magnetism rub off onto the candles.

Using the pen, write your name on the pink candle and your lover's name on the red candle. Place the candles in two holders set about seven inches apart. Light the candles and slide them slowly toward each other so that the candleholders touch, while you say,

*You are moving closer to me and returning*
*While these two candles are burning.*

Look into the flames, then close your eyes and visualise you and your lover laughing together.

Write your name on one bay leaf and your lover's name on another. Put a little cat fur on the bay leaf that bears your lover's name. Place the bay leaf with your name on top of the fur. The names should face each other. Your cat's static fur will draw your lover back to you. Keep the bay leaves together with two paperclips. Put the leaves in an envelope. Snuff out the candle, and sleep with the envelope under your pillow or inside your pillowcase.

# A MAGICAL MIRROR
# LOVE REFLECTION SPELL

*You will need:*

- One pink candle
- A hand mirror or dressing table mirror
- Seven rose buds
- Seven cloves
- A handkerchief or unused envelope
- About a six-inch length of pink ribbon

Sit with your cat and stroke your cat until he purrs; then hold a mirror to your cat's nose so that his breath makes the mirror misty. Put your cat on your bed while you light the pink candle. Drop the rose buds and cloves into the centre of a handkerchief, and tie the cloth into a ball shape with the pink ribbon; alternatively, place them in the envelope and tie the ribbon around it.

Pick up your cat and sit so that you are both looking into the mirror, then say,

> *Magic mirror in front of the wall,*
> *Attract one in true love with me to fall.*
> *May we bring out good in each other*
> *And may I find a faithful lover.*

Continue to cuddle your cat before snuffing out the candle. Sleep with the tied handkerchief or envelope inside your pillowcase or carry the handkerchief or envelope close to your skin.

# CHAPTER 4

# Spells for Happiness & Luck

In life, do your best and try to be happy. Always keep a sense of humour. Follow your intuition because it is your inner compass that points you in the right direction to do the right thing. The word intuition literally means "to be taught from within."

Relaxing with your cat helps you de-stress, and when you are calm, like your cat, it is easier to tune in to your inner soul and essential nature.

# TO TRANSFORM BAD LUCK TO GOOD

*The number eight symbolizes union. You will need:*

- Four stalks of wheat, oats,
  or barley straw
- Thread or string

Take the four stalks of straw, and twist them in opposite directions in a figure eight. Tie the ends of the straw with thread.

Put the figure eight inside your cat's basket and keep it there.

Every time you see your cat jump out of or into her basket, say,

*Cat jump out, cat jump in,*
*Bad luck out and good luck in.*

Alternatively, place the figure eight on the floor and play with your cat so that she jumps through it or puts her paws through it. If the straw breaks, it does not matter.

When you no longer have use for the talisman, bury it or throw it in a stream, river, or the sea.

It is said to be lucky to have a cat living in a theatre. It is an ill omen if a cat enters the stage during a performance. To have a black cat in the audience on opening night is good luck.

# TO MAKE SOMETHING SPECIAL HAPPEN

*You will need:*

- One candle
- A straight pin
- An acorn

Hold the candle in front of your cat so that your familiar scratches it with her paws. Inscribe on the candle, using the pin, what it is you wish to happen. Insert the pin through the wick from right to left. Put the candle in the east on a table, and light it while holding the acorn in your hand and saying,

> *As the pin pierces the wick,*
> *It will work a magical trick.*
> *My inscription on the wax*
> *Will bring me [and speak what it is that you want].*

While still holding the acorn, sit with the candle until it burns through the pin and inscription. Snuff out the candle and bury the candle stub and pin in an easterly position outdoors.

# FOR GOOD WEATHER ON A SPECIAL DAY

*Cats dislike rain and can help drive it away. This spell requires no supplies. When your cat is sitting high or basking in a beam of sunlight, say,*

> *[Day of the week] is my special day,*
> *Pussycat keep the rain away.*
> *May you make the sun shine,*
> *May [day of the week] be fine.*

Look at a cloud in the sky, and decide in your mind to bore a hole through the cloud to reveal blue sky or to make the cloud move to the left or right. Stare at the cloud while you think it, and you will see for yourself that the cloud does move according to your command.

# TO ENCOURAGE YOUR PARENTS TO RECONCILE AND REUNITE

*Sometimes feuding loved ones need a little help to get past their differences. You will need:*

- A little naturally shed cat fur
- A photo of your mother
- A photo of your father
- A few paper clips
- A tiger's-eye stone

Place some cat's fur between a photo of your mother and a photo of your father. The photos should be positioned face to face and held together with paper clips. Place a tiger's-eye stone on top of the photos, and keep the photos with the stone on top among your personal possessions for as long as necessary.

*If your cat cries, dashes around, and seems shocked for no apparent reason, he is telling you that a family argument is about to occur.*

# FOR HELP TO PASS A TEST OR EXAM

*The spirit world will help you to pass your exam as long as you do your bit by working and studying for it. On the day of the exam, say a prayer for the right answers to come into your mind. If you can't find a catnip plant (Nepeta cataria), use a catnip cat toy instead. You will need:*

- Some catnip
- A handkerchief or scrap of cloth, or a clean piece of paper
- A length of red ribbon or string
- An unused envelope (optional)

Take a handful of catnip leaf. Hold it in your hand and you will find that the catnip warms up. Place the catnip on a handkerchief or piece of paper.

Hold your cat's paws in your two hands while they are still warm. You will probably find that your cat tries to nuzzle her nose into your clasped hands pushing them apart. At the moment you open your hands, say,

*I will pass my [name of] exam.*

Tie the catnip into the handkerchief using the red ribbon or string, or place the paper with the catnip in an envelope and tie the ribbon around the envelope.

Place the handkerchief inside your pillowcase, and each night before going to sleep say,

*I will pass my [name of] exam.*

On the day of your exam, carry the catnip handkerchief with you. Afterward, give it to your cat to use as a toy.

# FOR A SUCCESSFUL JOB INTERVIEW

*Basil is an herb that attracts wealth. You will need:*

- A cat's whisker
- A basil plant in a pot or in the garden
- Lipstick
- Your interview letter
- A piece of unused paper

When your cat is in your kitchen, show her the letter asking you to attend a job interview. Put lipstick on your cat's right front paw. Encourage your cat to walk onto the letter to make a lipstick paw print and then another paw print on a clean piece of paper. Bury the piece of paper in the soil in which the basil plant is growing. Insert your cat's whisker into the soil.

Use the basil in your cooking, or eat a leaf every day before your job interview. The herb will nourish the bond you share with your cat and will attract the job you are seeking. Carry the interview letter in your purse to your job interview.

# TO INCREASE YOUR POPULARITY

*The Egyptian ankh, a cross with a loop, represents eternal life. You will need:*

- One beetroot
- A fountain pen with a nib
- A clean piece of paper

Place the beet in a pot with enough water to cover it, and bring to a boil. Reduce the heat and simmer for about an hour until it is soft. Leave it and the water to cool. Remove the beet, rub the skin, and eat it. Do not discard the cooking water.

Fill the fountain pen with the water in which you boiled the beet. Write your name, followed by the names of people whom you already know and would like to see or be involved with more often. After their names, draw the sign of the ankh. Fold the paper to conceal the writing and the symbol.

When your familiar is resting, rub the piece of paper from the tip of her nose down her spine to the tip of her tail and then kiss your cat's nose while saying,

> *This sign in Egyptian*
> *Is a prescription*
> *For me blending,*
> *Friendship unending.*

Bury the piece of paper in the soil of a potted plant or under a tree or garden plant. You will find that the people whose names you wrote will include you in their social lives.

# TO BRING PEACE OF MIND

*No animal understands the healing power of sleep and relaxation better than the cat. You will need:*

- A cat's whisker or some naturally shed fur
- A handkerchief or pouch
- Lavender flowers
- Chamomile flowers
- A short length of ribbon

Put your cat's naturally shed whisker or fur into a handkerchief with lavender and chamomile flowers. Tie them in place and put the bundle inside your pillowcase; their scent will help you sleep.

When you lie in bed, close your eyes and tell your guardian angel what problem you would like solved. Say "thank you" in the knowledge that you have already received what it is you are asking for.

You will find that the jigsaw pieces of your life start slotting into place. You will have peace of mind knowing that you are able to call for help whenever you feel in need of assistance or comfort.

# TO KNOW YOUR CAT IS HAPPY
# WHILE YOU ARE AWAY

*This spell works two ways: to bring joy to your holiday and to maintain your link to your cat while you are away. You will need:*

- A drop of milk in your cat's bowl
- A piece of paper with the name of
  your travel destination written on it.
- One candle, green or golden or white
- A photograph of your cat
- An unused envelope

Dip your cat's paw into the milk, and press her paw onto the piece of paper on which you have written your holiday destination. Light the candle and hold the piece of paper at a safe distance above the candle flame. The heat of the flame will turn the paw print brown.

Put the piece of paper and a photograph of your cat in the envelope and snuff out the candle. Put the envelope inside your suitcase or travel bag to take on holiday with you.

While away, look at the photograph of your cat and send love to her by thought.

# TO KEEP INTRUDERS AWAY

*Your cat is territorial, so you can reinforce boundary lines with the help of your familiar. Garlic is ruled by the planet Mars, which protects from theft. You will need:*

- One head of garlic
- A pot of soil or a garden
- Some fur from your cat's brush or a discarded whisker or claw sheath

Separate the cloves from the head of garlic. Take the pot of soil and bury some of your cat's fur, along with a discarded whisker or claw sheath if you have them. Press the cloves of garlic into the soil and cover them with dirt.

Hold your cat and press one of her front paws into the soil to make one or more paw prints. Afterward, stroke your cat's whiskers or ears and say,

> *I stroke your whiskers*
> *And I stroke your ears.*
> *We have no fears.*
> *No intruder nears.*
> *All harmful people are kept away, at bay.*

The garlic cloves you have planted will multiply into bulbs, increasing the protective force around your home. If you potted the garlic cloves, keep the pot or pots beside your front or back door inside or out, or alternatively on a windowsill that faces east (where the sun rises).

# CHAPTER 5

# Spells for Wealth & Good Fortune

There is nothing wrong with having money except what you would do to get it and how you would use it once you have it.

Mercury, the planet closest to the sun, relates to gold and wealth, and for this reason money spells often seek to tap into its energy. Money spells are often performed on Wednesdays, the day of the week governed by Mercury. The fluid and dynamic character of Mercury has an unlimited capacity for transformation. Mercury also symbolises your subconscious and will attract wealth to you because you need it. Because Mercury is the planet of wealth, if you link to its energy successfully do not doubt that the money you need will arrive—sometimes immediately, other times not. I think the timing may also depend on whether we ourselves are at a high or low ebb. Sometimes we are more in sync than at others.

# TO ATTRACT MONEY INTO
# YOUR HOME AND LIFE

*This spell is particularly effective for attracting money to you quickly.
It should be cast on a Wednesday. Because the waxing moon enhances
growth in your life, cast your spell when the moon is new, visible as a
crescent in the sky, with the horns pointing to the left. You will need:*

- One golden candle
- One silver candle
- Fur from your cat's brush
- Two saucers or small dishes
- Loose change, uncounted
- Inside front doormat
- A $10 bill
- Cat toy
- A pen
- Green paper

Light the golden candle to represent the sun and the silver candle to represent Mercury, quicksilver.

Brush your cat while you tell him that you would like him to help bring money into your life as quickly as possible, not for greed but by necessity. Remove strands of his fur from the brush, and place them in a saucer between the two candles. Put all your loose change in the saucer. Avoid calculating how much the coins add up to because that would limit your expectations.

Take your cat to the doormat inside the main entrance of your home and let him see you place the $10 bill under the doormat. Throw one of your cat's toys onto the doormat to entice him to leap onto the doormat. Whatever money you place under the mat must be left there until a Full Moon, so deposit the largest amount you can afford.

With your cat beside you, sit in front of the candles and coins. On a piece of green paper, write everything you need the money for.

Burn the piece of paper by passing it first through the flame of the golden candle and next through the flame of the silver candle. Leave the paper to extinguish in a second saucer. Determine how many hours the candles should burn based on how many money wishes you have. Every hour represents one wish. If you have three money wishes, let the candles burn in your presence for three hours before snuffing them out.

Gather the coins and return them to your purse or wallet or to wherever they were before you began casting your spell. Only remove the bill from under your doormat when the moon is full or waning; otherwise you may invite expense. During the time the bill is under the mat, any visitor to your home will attract wealth to you by stepping on the doormat.

# TO ATTRACT A SPECIFIC
# AMOUNT OF MONEY

*This spell uses colour symbolism to work its magic. Red is the colour of blood, the life force; gold is the colour of wealth and high spirituality. You will need:*

- A piece of scrap paper and a pen or pencil
- A pen with red ink
- A small piece of gold paper or a gold card
- A photograph of your cat

On the piece of scrap paper, write in capital letters the figure you need, for instance, TEN THOUSAND DOLLARS.

Delete all letters that are repeated in the words—in this case, the Ts, Ns, Os, Ss, As, Ds, and Ls. The letters that don't recur are H, E, U, and R (which sound rather like "here you are").

Write the letters H E U R in cursive script with the letters attached using red ink on a small piece of gold paper or a gold card. Place the card, face-to-face, with a picture of your cat, in your purse or wallet. Keep it there to speed money to you.

When I cast this spell, I received the exact amount I asked for—two years later! I had forgotten about it until the gold paper came to my attention when I was transferring the contents of an old wallet to a new one.

# TO SPEED CASH TO YOU QUICKLY

*You will need:*

- Some cash, any denomonations
- Catnip (optional)
- About a six-inch strand of gold-coloured thread
- A jar or pot

Put a pile of cash on the floor. Get your cat to rub his paws into it by sprinkling catnip over it. Alternatively, play with the coins to entice your cat to join in and touch the coins with his paws or body.

Roll the paper money into a cylinder, and secure it with the gold thread. Keep the money scroll in your purse and do not spend it.

Put the pile of coins that you have sprinkled with catnip into a pot. Keep the pot in the eastern part of your home and do not spend the cash. Because the east is where the sun rises, every day you will attract new money into your home.

# TO GET OUT OF DEBT

*This spell must begin on the night the moon is full. You will need:*

- Nine ice cubes
- A dish
- Water from your cat's bowl
- Nine new, disposable cleaning cloths
- Nine drops camphor oil

On the night of a full moon, call your familiar to you in the kitchen. Keep your cat with you in the kitchen while you put nine ice cubes into a dish. Pour a little water from your cat's bowl over the ice. Sprinkle the ice with nine drops of camphor oil. When the ice has melted, converse with your cat, telling him precisely what debt you would like him to help you clear. Clean your stove by wiping the camphor and water solution with a brand-new cloth. Throw the cloth away afterward and then play and talk with your cat.

Cast your spell again on the following eight consecutive nights. Keep your familiar in the kitchen, talking to him while melting the ice and cleaning the stove again. Each night, use a new cloth soaked in the water from the nine ice cubes melted with nine drops of camphor oil. The ice symbolically takes the heat out of the volatile situation represented by the camphor. The stove relates to your nourishment. If you cannot cast your spell on each of the nine nights, clean your stove during the day instead, but do not miss any 24-hour period.

Before long, well-paid work, a windfall, or a check will arrive, enabling you to clear your debt. You may also find your debtor partially writing off the debt.

# TO DOUBLE YOUR MONEY

*Green represents wealth. You will need:*

- A small piece of ginger root
- One of your cat's shed claws or
  a dressmaking pin
- A gold-coloured coin
- A small length of green ribbon
  or thread

Into the ginger root, insert a claw your cat has shed; alternatively, use a dressmaking pin. Bind the gold-coloured coin to the ginger with green ribbon or thread. Keep the amulet in a secret place.

Three days before a full moon, put the amulet on a windowsill or carry it to a position where it is exposed to the moon. Repeat this on the night before the full moon and on the night of the full moon. Return the amulet to its secret place.

By the time of the new moon (it always occurs two weeks after the full moon) you will find that your financial good fortune has doubled.

# TO SELL YOUR HOME
# FOR THE RIGHT PRICE

*Before starting this spell, have a word with your cat and tell him that you want the right buyer to come along and offer you the price you want for the home that you or your family is selling. You will need:*

- One green candle
- A cat toy or small length of string

With your familiar beside you, light the green candle. When your cat is in the mood to be picked up, carry him to one of the walls in the room in which you are standing. Dangle one of his toys or a piece of string against the wall so that your cat taps the wall with his paw. Your cat may be happy for you to hold his paw and tap the wall with it. After your cat has tapped the wall, speak aloud the price you wish for your home.

Carry your cat or encourage him to follow you into every room of your home and tap a wall in each place. When your cat has tapped the wall with his paw, speak aloud the desired price for your home.

Symbolically, cats are the guardians of marriage. That is why in England brides sometimes carried a black cat along with their wedding bouquet.

# TO PREVENT LEGAL ACTION

*This spell is specifically designed to safeguard your assets against legal action. You will need:*

- Seven dried beans
- A crossroads

When your familiar is comfortably settled, seat yourself beside him and put seven dried beans in your mouth. Spit the beans out while speaking the name of the entity or person who is threatening legal action against you.

Pick up the beans and drop them onto your cat saying,

*Beloved cat, I have spat out the beans*
*And will keep what is mine, by honest means.*

Using your fingers, remove the beans from your cat, or pick up your cat so that the beans fall to the floor.

Take the beans to a crossroads and throw them over your left shoulder without looking backward. As you throw them, think or say aloud,

*[Name or entity, entities, person, or people], my cat [his name] and I command you, begone.]*

Walk away and do not look back.

That night, take your cat to bed with you and hold him. Speak aloud to tell God, or the spirit world, what your problem is and then ask that higher power to deal with your problem for you. From then on, all you need do is deal with the impending legal situation as the time demands. Purposely do not think of your problem in the meantime, because deprived of the fuel of your thoughts, the problem will dissipate.

# TO RECEIVE MONEY YOU ARE OWED

*Star anise is a spice that is sold at specialty foods stores and super-markets. You will need:*

- One stick of lavender incense in a holder
- A little milk in your cat's bowl
- Four whole star anise pods
- One white candle
- A fountain pen or pen with a nib
- A small piece of white paper
- An unused envelope (optional)

With your familiar at your side, light the lavender incense. Put your cat's bowl, containing a little milk, beside the incense. Place the four star anise pods around the white candle, and then light the candle. Look into the candle flame and say,

> *[Name of corporation or person] you will pay me the money that you owe me.*
> *I give thanks that I have already received it.*

Fill the fountain pen with milk or dip a pen nib into the milk. Write on the piece of white paper the name of the person or corporation owing you the money. Beneath the name, write the owed amount.

Hold the piece of paper near the candle flame, and watch the words and amount that you have written in milk turn brown from the heat. Hold the piece of paper and visualise receiving the money.

When the incense has finished burning, blow out the candle. Fold the piece of paper into three. Throw the remainder of the milk in your cat's bowl away, and fill the bowl with fresh water or milk. Keep the piece of paper under your cat's drinking bowl until the money owed to you is repaid. Put the star anise in an envelope to carry in your purse to speed the money's arrival.

Continue to light the white candle every day until it burns to a stub. If you have an open hearth, burn the candle stub. If not, bury the candle stub.

Once the money owed has been paid, bury the star anise and piece of paper that bears the debtor's name and the owed amount.

# CHAPTER 6

# Spells for Health & Healing

*C*harms and spells for health have been used for centuries. Being fortunate enough to live in an age of advanced medicine, we rely on them less. But when performed hand in hand with medicine, healing spells can still do good to people and to pets.

The ancient Egyptians believed that cats helped to keep illness away from the home because they kill snakes and vermin. Japanese folk traditions say that a cat placed on an ill person's stomach can cure the person. Cat fur has been used in old folk remedies to aid the healing of scalds, burns, and rheumatism. Rheumatic people encouraged a cat to sit on their lap or sleep with them, for the cat to relieve them of the pain. Some thought that their own pain was transferred to the cat.

In Egyptian tradition, the cat was believed to be the possessor of life because of her connection to the sun-eye and to the sun god Horus, who was the source of good health and happiness. Cat amulets guard the health and safely protect the wearer or property in which the amulet is placed. Egyptian cat talismans also protected the dead. Most of the spells in this chapter are to be worked by you and your cat in partnership, but a few provide ways for you to protect your cat's health and well-being.

# TO HEAL YOUR CAT

*Bay leaves, ruled by the sun, represent triumph over adversity. You will need:*

- Modeling clay
- Fur from your cat's brush
- A rose quartz crystal (alternatively, a red stone or a red rose or red flower in bloom)
- A bay leaf

Using modeling clay, make a little "poppet" to resemble your ailing cat. Try to make the model look as much like her as possible. Press some of her brushed-out fur into the modeling clay.

Press the rose quartz into the heart area on the left-hand side of the cat model's chest, thinking as you do so that you wish your cat well. Rose quartz is used because it represents love, associated with the heart, and because quartz transmits heat, rays, light, and ultraviolet rays. If you cannot get a rose quartz, find a small shiny red pebble or stone. A fresh rose, renewed when it wilts, would also serve your purpose.

Kiss the fresh bay leaf and place your cat model upon it. All cats love the sun, so place the leaf and model in a comfortable position in your home, where the sun will shine on it.

# TO HEAL YOUR CAT WHEN
# YOU ARE APART

*Use this spell when your cat is at the vet's, when you are on holiday, or even when you are just away from home for a few hours. You will need:*

- A magnifying glass
- A photograph of your cat

Hold the magnifying glass an inch or two above the photograph of your cat. You may be quite startled to see that the cat in the photograph appears to come to life. Send strong healing thoughts to your familiar while looking through the magnifying glass and, if you like, also speak to wish her well. Your words have a vibration and resonance that reach much farther than hearing distance.

*If your cat sneezes once, you will be kissed by a stranger.*
*Two sneezes, you will receive something good.*
*Three sneezes, you will have a cold in three days.*
*Four sneezes are an omen of marriage.*
*Five sneezes predict the birth of a baby boy.*
*Six sneezes forecast the birth of a girl.*
*Seven sneezes means you will live a long and fulfilled life.*

# TO AID YOUR CAT DURING
# A VISIT TO THE VET

*The veterinarian's office can be a frightening place. This spell can help your cat be more receptive to the kind of healing offered by the vet. You will need:*

- A cut glass crystal or prism,
  to reflect rainbow colours

Stroke your familiar to calm her down. The tactile warmth of your hand stroking her fur, by its soothing effect, helps to heal you and her at the same moment and creates a bond.

Move the crystal above your cat's body, to shine coloured light over your cat's heart. Hold the crystal still for a few moments, then hold the crystal above your cat's head. Focus on sending healing energy into your familiar through the light refracted by the crystal.

Move the crystal from the tip of your cat's nose, over her head and down her spine to the tip of your cat's tail and say,

*You are well you are healed from nose to tail and from tip to toe*

As you are saying "from tip to toe" move the crystal from your cat's head down to her spine, and from there down all four legs to each paw.

End the spell by holding the crystal over the palm of your other hand so that the colours of the rainbow appear as light upon your own skin.

If either you or your cat is injured or has had an operation, you can aid healing by holding the crystal to the wound for a few minutes, so that light shines through the crystal onto the injury or surgical incision.

Afterward, place the crystal inside your pillowcase and sleep with your cat on top of your pillow.

# TO HEAL A PERSON IN YOUR PRESENCE

*A spell like this, worked in front of another person, is best done when your cat has had some experience of doing magical work with you. You will need:*

- A piece of paper
- A pen or pencil
- A ball of wool

Place your cat on the lap of the person who is unwell, or put your cat beside the person you wish to heal.

Write the name of the person's illness on a piece of paper. Scrunch the piece of paper up. Roll a ball of wool around the piece of paper. Give the ball of wool to your cat to bat with her paws and chase out the door of the room where the unwell person is sitting in.

Afterward, unravel the ball of wool and burn or bury the piece of paper.

# LONG-DISTANCE HEALING

*When a far-away someone you care about is ill, you and your familiar can help. You will need:*

- One white or blue candle
- An upright mirror

Place a candle in front of an upright mirror, such as a dressing-table mirror, making sure that the candle cannot ignite anything. Settle your cat close to you and light the candle. Hold your cat in your arms so that the mirror reflects both of you together. Look into your cat's eyes, reflected in the mirror and say,

> *In the candle flame burning brightly tonight,*
> *[Name of cat] and I send you healing light.*
> *We wish you well, we want you to be.*
> *Get well soon, from Kitty and me.*

If at any point your cat wishes to be free from your arms, let her jump down. Continue, with or without your cat, to look in the mirror and visualise the one who is ill made well and happy. By mental telepathy send the light reflected in the mirror to the person whom you are healing.

When you are ready, snuff out the candle.

# TO HEAL A BROKEN HEART

*The candle in this spell represents the person whose heart you are trying to heal. You will need:*

- A sheet of paper cut into two small pieces
- A pen (not ballpoint)
- A teaspoonful or two of distilled vinegar in a small dish
- Several drops of rose oil
- Another small dish
- One blue or white candle

Write on one of the pieces of paper: "Heal [name of the person]'s broken heart." Drop the piece of paper into the dish of vinegar and watch the ink spread and change colour. Light the candle and say,

*All bitterness has gone from [name of person].*

Write on another piece of paper: "[Name of person], whose broken heart is to be healed." Drop the piece of paper into a clean dish. Sprinkle the piece of paper with a few drops of rose oil and say,

*It is a grace and a gift that [name of person] has forgiven.*
*[Name of person]'s broken heart is healed and they have love in their heart.*

Snuff out the candle. Outdoors, bury the piece of paper from the vinegar dish, pouring the vinegar away. Keep the piece of paper on which you sprinkled the rose oil. Give the piece of paper to the person whose broken heart you have healed, to drop into their bathwater, or drop it into your own bathwater. Tear the piece of paper into tiny pieces to go down the drain with the bathwater.

# TO HEAL YOUR HOME
# OF NEGATIVE ENERGY

*You will need:*

- Your cat's collar with a bell on it,
  a cat toy with a bell inside, or a
  handbell
- One red candle

When your familiar is sitting with her paws on your shoulder, whisper into her left ear what it is that you wish to send out of your home. Then whisper in your cat's right ear what it is that you wish to welcome in.

Ask your cat to follow you into every room of your home, or carry your cat, if she is willing, into every room. In each of the four corners of each room, tinkle the bell on her collar, or remove your cat's collar and shake it in every corner. The ringing bell will dissipate stagnant energies and resonate differently in every room because of the quality of energies at different moments in time. The harmony of the bell will attract good fortune.

Light the red candle in a safe place, close to the door where your cat usually enters your home. When the flame is established, say,

*With each dainty velvet paw*
*Take bad luck away, out through the door.*
*And wherever you may roam,*
*Return with good luck for our home.*

Do not leave the candle unattended. When your cat goes out through the door, snuff out the candle. This spell can be cast indoors if you have a window through which you can see the moon.

# TO HEAL A RELATIONSHIP

*This spell must be performed when the moon is visible—preferably a new moon. You will need:*

- A hand mirror

Sit outside at dusk, if possible, with your cat on your lap. Hold the hand mirror so that it reflects the moon. Look at your cat's eyes and watch the pupils expand from horizontal slits until they look like two full moons.

Show your cat her reflection and the moon's reflection in the mirror and say,

> *Lady Moon of kindness and light,*
> *Heal my relationship with [name of person tonight].*
> *And may sunshine at the break of day*
> *Bring happiness again, our way.*

Kiss your cat and go indoors with your familiar and the mirror.

*If your cat climbs a tree on the day of a death or funeral, he is telling you that the departed soul has gone to heaven.*

# CHAPTER 7

# Felidomancy: Feline Divination

The Egyptian word for cat is *mau*, meaning "to see." Possessing divine powers and attuned with invisible energy, your cat shows you visible signs by his actions, eyes, body language, moods, and behaviour. Your cat is psychic and can help you to become psychic. His body language is an action to a reaction to magical knowledge. If you intuitively understand your cat, you can intuitively understand the divine nature of the universe.

You know that your familiar has your best interests at heart and in his wisdom knows what is best for you, tells you, and expects to be heard, simply because it is well deserved by both of you. Through your familiar you can tune in to your own omniscience, meaning all knowing, and know it all.

By linking into your cat, you too can see as a seer what is evident and what is not. Your cat is a seer, meaning that he can see the clear truth in a situation. Your cat can see in the dark.

The pupils of your cat's eyes are small in the morning and gradually enlarge during the day until they look like full moons at night. Follow your cat's wisdom: broaden your outlook. Your familiar will sit with his eyes fixed upon you until you look back and acknowledge his glare. When eye contact is established, you will understand the wordless psychic contact that makes you stop and think, see and understand what your cat is telling you.

# YES OR NO DIVINATION

- Seat your cat on your lap, and tell your familiar that you wish him to divine your future by answering a question you are about to ask aloud. Ask your familiar to respond by blinking once if the answer to your question is yes, twice for no. Alternatively, ask your familiar to purr an odd number of times for yes and an even number of times for no.

- To find the answer to a yes or no question, brush or stroke your cat's tail. Place three hairs from his tail on a piece of paper. Fold up the paper so that the hairs cannot fall out. Put the folded paper under your pillow and sleep on it. In the morning open the paper. If the three hairs are in the shape of the initial Y the answer to your question is yes. Any shape other than a Y, answers no to your question. Sometimes the answer comes in a dream while the amulet is under your pillow.

- Write a question that requires a yes or no answer on a small piece of paper. Write your cat's name above and below and on either side of the question. Scrunch the piece of paper into a ball, and place it inside a poppy-seed pod. Put the poppy-seed pod inside your pillowcase, and the yes or no answer that you seek will be revealed to you in a dream.

- Give a pomegranate to your cat to play with and chase after, as if it were a ball. When you are ready to know a yes or no answer to a question that you have in mind, take the pomegranate outdoors. Throw the pomegranate hard on the ground so that it smashes and the seeds fall out. (Be sure to do this on the dirt, not a paved area, and to wear dark-coloured clothing, since pomegranate juice stains.) Pick up the pomegranate seeds from the ground and count them.

An even number of seeds answers yes to your question. An odd number of seeds answers no to your question.

- Write your yes or no question on a piece of paper, and scrunch the piece of paper into a ball that your cat will bat with his paw. Play with your cat to entice him to chase the ball of paper. If your familiar bats the paper ball more often with his right paw, the answer to your question is yes. The answer is no if he bats the ball of paper more often with his left paw. Alternatively, sit opposite your cat and roll the ball of paper toward him so that he bats it back to you. An even number of times that your cat bats the ball back to you answers yes. An odd number of times answers no to your question.

- Take an oak leaf. Dip it into the water in your cat's bowl. Show the leaf to him and ask him to lick the leaf. Place the leaf on a piece of paper. If the leaf dries slowly, the answer is yes. If the leaf dries quickly, the answer is no.

- Your familiar will tell you the answer to your yes or no question if you listen to him drinking his milk or water. With your question in mind, count how many laps your cat takes. An even number divines the answer yes; an odd number signifies no.

- Take thirteen little scraps of paper torn from a single sheet of paper. Write the word yes on six pieces and the word no on seven pieces. Scrunch each piece of paper into a small ball. Hold all thirteen wads of paper in your hand and rattle them to encourage your cat to make you open your hand so they fall to the floor. Alternatively, place the wads of paper in a pile on the floor and dangle string over them so that your cat leaps onto them, scattering the pile. Pick up the wad that lands farthest away from the others. Smooth the piece of paper in your hand, and read yes or no in answer to your question.

# HE LOVES ME, HE LOVES ME NOT

Place a small handful of cat treats in your cat's dish. After your familiar has eaten, count the number of treats your familiar leaves. With each treat you count, read one line. The line that coincides with the final treat gives you your answer.

*[first treat] He loves me.*
*[second treat] He loves me not.*
*[third treat ] He'll want me.*
*[fourth treat] He won't.*
*[fifth treat] If he could he would.*
*[sixth treat] But he can't.*

# WILL I GET WHAT I WANT?

Pour some cat treats into your familiar's dish, and leave them there to be eaten. When you later visit your familiar's treat bowl, count the remaining treats speaking one line for each treat counted:

*[first treat] I will get what I want.*
*[second treat] I won't get what I want.*

Continue until the last line spoken with the last treat gives you your answer.

# IS HE A GOOD GUY?

Being highly sensitive, your feline friend can intuitively read a person's character. Your cat's tail will tell you what he thinks of a person. If the tail and tip are up, your cat is saying that he likes the person. Your familiar also approves if his tail curves down with the tip up. If your familiar's tail is slightly raised and slightly curved, your cat is interested without fear. If your cat's tail is up with the tip tilted, he is interested in your friend, but also wary.

It is a sign that a person irritates your familiar if your cat twitches the tip of his tail. When your cat lowers his tail or tucks it behind his hind legs, he is telling you that he feels intimidated by the person. If your familiar arches and bristles his tail, he feels threatened.

Your familiar is telling you that he is fearful if he fluffs out his tail fur. If your cat holds his tail up and the tail fur is fluffed up too, your cat is telling you that he strongly disapproves of the person you have introduced to him.

Another sign that your familiar disapproves of someone is if he washes vigorously when meeting the person.

# HYDROMANCY

To find which of three potential partners would make you happiest or which of three people will ask you out, ask your cat to reveal the answer with a little hydromancy.

Partially fill three identical bowls with water. Place a bay leaf in one bowl to represent one lover, a rose petal in the second dish to represent the second sweetheart, and an oak leaf in the third bowl to symbolize the third suitor.

The bowl your cat drinks from reveals the one most compatible with you, or as the case may be, the one who will ask you for a date.

# FELINE WEATHER FORECASTS

Your cat is able to predict how the weather will change within the next few hours. If you read your familiar's signs, you can plan accordingly:

- If your familiar sharpens his claws on the furniture, good weather is on its way.
- "Cat on its brain is a sign of rain." Expect rain if your familiar curls up with the back of his head between his ears, flat on the furniture or floor, with his chin in the air.
- If your cat licks his feet, head, and whiskers, then over and behind his ears, rain will soon fall.
- When your cat sneezes once, expect a rain shower.
- It is also said to be a forecast of rain if your cat sits staring out of the window.
- Sailors draw omens from a cat's behaviour. "Cat's paw" is a nautical expression meaning a light breeze.
- A cat mewing on board is a sign of a gale.
- A cat scratching on wood, such as a door frame or table leg, or even its own scratching post, is a sign of rough weather, because the cat is thought to be "raising a storm."
- High winds and storms are forecast if your cat frolics and jumps as if suddenly bitten by a flea.
- "The cat has a gale of wind in his tail." Anticipate gales and storms if your cat is frisky and twitches his tail quickly.
- If your cat sits with his tail to the fire, it is an omen of frost and a spell of cold weather.

# ARE YOU FAMILIAR WITH
# YOUR FAMILIAR?

*The "eyes" have it:* Cats' pupils shine in the dark and reflect light at dawn and dusk, as well as in low light. "Cat's-eye," the semiprecious opalescent mineral gem, has acquired its name because it possesses chatoyancy, changing shine and colour, like cats' eyes in the dark.

Cats are nocturnal hunters, and their eyes glow in the dark because they absorb more light than human eyes. Unlike humans, cats have a mirror-like layer behind the retina that reflects light to the retinal cells.

*By a whisker:* Your familiar has twelve whiskers in four horizontal rows on each side of his nose. The twenty-four whiskers are more than sensitive detectors that tell a cat whether a gap is wide enough for his body to enter and exit without getting stuck; they are surrounded by nerve endings that detect air currents and solid objects without contact, enabling your familiar to hunt, as skillfully by night as by day. When cats hunt they wind their whiskers around their prey to detect whether the victim is dead or alive.

Your familiar moves his whiskers forward when inquisitive and backward when wary. The top two rows can move in unison and out of sync with the bottom two rows, and the middle rows are the most sensitive of all.

*Purring:* Cats begin purring as week-old kittens to let their mother cat know they are receiving the milk she is feeding them. She responds by purring back. Cats in a friendly, contented mood purr to say they feel sociable, as well as to say thank you. But cats in pain also purr to ask for help.

*The cat's meow:* A cat's meow is said to consist of sixty-three notes. This may be the origin of lore about communication between a witch and her familiar. The witch's cat was said to speak the language of its mistress. One witch, Moll White, owned a tabby who was reputed to have spoken in English on several occasions.

*Cat tails:* The Greek word for cat means "tail waver." Your familiar waves his tail from side to side when he is feeling indecisive.

*Cat tail cures:* The tip of your cat's tail brushed on a wart is said to make it wither and disappear.

It is believed that a sty on the eyelid will disappear quickly if you brush it with the tip of a black cat's tail while reciting this age-old saying,

> *I poke thee,*
> *I don't poke thee.*
> *I poke the queff that's under the ee*
> *O qualway, qualway.*

# YOUR CAT'S AURA

Your cat has an aura, or glowing emanation. About an inch from his body you will see white or golden light. Beyond that, still flowing in the shape of your cat, is a misty color extending outward about twelve inches.

A change of mood can alter your cat's aura from one colour to another, until his state of mind returns to its usual disposition. A zigzag flash, similar to a lightning flash, can appear in your familiar's aura if something suddenly excites, shocks, or frightens him.

The colours and key words listed below tell you your cat's nature and what he predicts about your immediate future.

RED: Your familiar is strong-willed, possessing a great love for life. He is passionate and very affectionate. A feral familiar with a red aura may suddenly become aggressive because red is the colour of blood and fire. *Key words: lusty, strong, courageous, powerful*

GOLD: The overruling nature of the cat whose aura is gold is goodness, intelligence, and consideration. In your familiar, you possess a treasure beyond earthly wealth because gold is the colour of the highest spirituality, as well as majesty. *Key words: divine, spiritual, healthy*

ORANGE: You have a precious and very special cat. He is uncommonly wise, affectionate, and cheerful, possessing a loving heart and a great sense of humour. Because orange is the colour of the sun, which brings illumination and life, your familiar will bring light and happiness into your life and home. *Key words: successful, happy, fun, cleansing*

YELLOW: Your familiar is highly intelligent and spiritual. Because yellow is the colour of the sun when it is warm but not dangerously hot, your familiar lifts your mood to a happier, brighter, more peaceful state of mind. *Key words: psychic, divinatory, wise, visionary, enlightening*

GREEN: Your cat has a kind, sweet, freedom-loving nature. He is emotionally independent because green is the colour of nature. More often than not, your cat will like to sit where he can see outdoors. Cats with green auras are procreators who make excellent parents and show cats because they like exhibiting their talents. *Key words: lucky, prosperous, beautiful, youthful, faithful*

BLUE: Your familiar is a natural healer who is warm, calm, loyal, and affectionate. He exchanges his knowledge with you because he has a deep desire for you to understand him better and more intimately. *Key words: healing, peaceful, relaxing, calming, teaching, guiding*

INDIGO: Your familiar loves peace and harmony and may often appear to focus on things in the room that are invisible to you. He is sensitive to your moods and acts in accordance to them. *Key words: powerful, spiritual, omnipotent, loving*

VIOLET: Your familiar is psychic, forever youthful, and eager to entertain new people in your home or welcome a change of residence and a change of routine. He will teach you things about yourself in a most uncanny way. *Key words: sensitive, pure, spiritually protective, sagely, affectionate*

BLACK: A black aura is a sign that your familiar has experienced sadness or danger and is in need of love, reassurance, and safety. *Key words: good luck, opposites, attraction, stability, endurance, strength*

SILVER: Your very spiritual familiar is extremely perceptive, possessing a strong love link to you and to the invisible world. By tuning in to your familiar you will find that you are in sync with destiny: the right people and situations will appear, bringing good fortune, unexpected luck, and precisely what you require at a particular time. *Key words: intuitive, honest, sensitive, strong, feminine, warm, loving, giving*

# MAGICAL CAT WISHING POUCHES

You and your cat divided by time and geographical distance can remain linked if you carry a magical cat wishing pouch. Through it you are bound as one because something that has been in contact with a person or animal retains that connection.

A magical cat wishing pouch is a little bag filled with herbs, spices, and various objects of symbolic or magical significance. Carry the wishing pouch in your purse or pocket, or sleep with it under your pillow. You must light a white candle to represent purity when filling your wishing pouch for the first time.

You could put the ingredients in a little cloth purse you already possess. Alternatively, you can make a wishing pouch by placing the ingredients in the centre of a handkerchief, gathering the cloth around them, and tying them up into a bundle with a ribbon or cord. Another method is to cut a circle of felt. Glue a much smaller circle of cardboard in the centre of the felt circle. Punch an even number of holes around the outer edge of the felt, and thread the ribbon or cord through them to make a drawstring pouch.

The ingredients for your pouch should include a hair from your head and fur from your cat's brush. You can also add teeth or claws, your familiar has naturally shed. By carrying your cat's personal teeth or claws, you are not severed from your cat even though you may be apart.

You will also need to add a little cat-like pebble or stone that you find, because you are attracted to it, when you are out for a walk.

You should put into the bag a lucky charm: a photograph of your cat or a small drawing that represents something that you know or feel about your cat or your cat's behaviour or astrological birth sign.

In addition to maintaining your connection with your cat when you are apart, the wishing pouch can be used for magic. For luck in love, you should insert a few dried rose petals or rose buds. To attract healthy communication, add some lavender or, if you prefer, a whole nutmeg. Whenever you wish for something to happen, write your wish in ink on a bay leaf and put the bay leaf into the wishing pouch. To attract love, add seven apple seeds and some thyme, if you have it. For sexual potency, add a few dried beans or an oak leaf. To increase your psychic powers, include a few star anise pods and peppermint or spearmint leaves. For protection and purification, add a sprig of rosemary or some dried rose-mary or a bay leaf.

*A kitten born on Michaelmas Eve, September 28, or on Michaelmas Day, September 29, at the end of blackberry season, was in Britain affectionately known as a Michaelmas kitten or a "blackberry cat." The owner of a Michaelmas kitten should expect it to be unusually playful and mischievous.*

# CHAPTER 8

# Know Your Cat by Her Astrological Sign

*y*ou can cast a spell according to your cat's astrological birth sign to join the two of you together as working magical partners, bonding your cat as your familiar. First thing in the morning and last thing at night, say good morning and speak good night to your cat. Your friendship and hers should be appreciated and not taken for granted by either of you.

The characteristics of each sign are described here, and for each sign there is a spell you can use to initiate your cat as your familiar. Also listed are stones you can both wear to link yourselves psychically; you can also choose a collar of the stone's colour for your cat.

If you know the date of your cat's birth you will know her birth sign, which would be the same astrological sign as for a person born on that date. If you buy or acquire a kitten, you can discover the birth sign by counting the number of weeks of her age backward to the date of birth. Kittens usually are taken from their mother cat at about six to eight weeks of age.

If you have no idea of your cat's date of birth, reading the following descriptions will help you determine whether your cat is ruled by an Air, Fire, Water, or Earth Sign, which in turn will help you deduce which is your cat's most probable birth sign.

# YOUR CAT IS RULED BY AIR IF:

Your familiar is lean, tense, perceptive, clever, nervous, humorous, attention seeking, and restless. She enjoys watching your activities, looking out the window or door, and watching television. Your familiar's mood is fickle and as changeable and difficult to grasp as the wind. She is paws up in the air at one minute and curled up asleep the next. An Air cat enjoys her own company one minute and being the star of the show the next. The Air Signs are Gemini, Libra, and Aquarius.

## GEMINI CAT (May 21–June 21)

*Key words: I instinctively know my intuition is correct.*
*Stones or collar colours: Agate, Turquoise*

Gemini cats are the perfect familiar, because they need a soul mate. They are fast learners, easily housebroken, good fun, playful, talkative, always active, and full of nervous energy. Being ruled by the planet Mercury, they dart around with mercurial speed and are full of surprises.

You get two for the price of one with dual-natured Gemini cats. They are inquisitive, versatile, loving, and highly intelligent. Their sharp minds make them entertaining because they love being the centre of attention. They are fussy, not greedy, for food and need variety in their diet. Because they enjoy life outdoors, when indoors they need plenty to amuse their mentally active brains. Love is the answer.

Gemini cats could go astray more often than other cats. They may follow you down the road and would like wearing a cat harness to accompany you on walks.

# BONDING SPELL FOR
# A GEMINI FAMILIAR

*Caraway, mint, and lavender are all ruled by the planet Mercury, which governs your Gemini familiar. Wednesday is ruled by the planet Mercury, so Wednesday would be the best day on which to cast your spell. You will need:*

- One yellow or gold candle
- A pen or straight pin
- A flower pot filled with potting soil
- A few lavender flower heads
- A handkerchief or scrap of cloth
- A few pinches of caraway seeds
- Some fur taken from your cat's brush
- A yellow ribbon or thread
- A mint plant

Writing lengthwise on the candle, inscribe with a pen or straight pin your cat's name, followed by your full name. Put the candle in the flower pot on the table. Settle your cat beside you and light the candle.

Strip the lavender heads, letting the buds fall into the centre of the handkerchief or scrap of cloth. Add the caraway seeds and cat fur. Lift the edges of the cloth up to tie the ingredients into a bundle using the yellow ribbon or thread.

Sit with the candle while it burns through both your inscribed names. Snuff the candle out.

Sleep that night with the bundle under your pillow and your cat on top of your bed. Afterward, keep the handkerchief among your personal possessions or close to you.

The following day, bury the candle stub in your garden and plant the mint on top of it. Alternatively, push the candle stub into the flower pot and plant the mint on top of it. As the mint thrives, so too will your bond with your familiar. The mint will keep your relationship fresh and lively.

# LIBRA CAT (September 23–October 23)

*Key words: Peace and harmony*
*Stone or collar colour: Opal*

Your Libra familiar is a brilliant companion for your spells because she is happiest being the fireside cat. Libra cats like a peaceful home. Because harmony and justice are essential to their nature, they are very loving, instinctively knowing what is fair to you and to them. They understand what you say to them and learn easily.

Libra cats have a clean, well-balanced, beautiful body and refined features. They like company and will be friendly to you, your friends, and other pets you may have. Their good looks, sociability, and need for pampering make them successful candidates for cat shows. They love being groomed.

Libra familiars are indecisive with food and find it hard to make up their minds about what tastes best. Although they may appear serene, they are inwardly nervous and need to be treated with sensitivity and kindness. They may react to household arguments by not eating a meal, because the stress of it has made them lose their appetite.

Should your familiar turn her attention to another member of the family, do not look on it as disloyalty. It is because she has so much love to give and wants everybody to be happy.

# BONDING SPELL FOR A LIBRA FAMILIAR

*Friday is governed by Venus, your familiar's ruling planet, so Friday would be the best day on which to cast a spell to unite you and your familiar as a magical working team. All the ingredients are also governed by the planet. You will need:*

- One pale blue or pale pink candle
- Two small pieces of paper
- A pen with blue ink
- Two red roses
- A vase filled with water
- An apple
- A straight pin
- A pear
- Pale pink or pale blue ribbon or thread

Settle your cat so that she is with you when you cast your spell. Light the candle and place it on a table. On one of the two small pieces of paper write your cat's name in cursive writing with the blue pen, followed by your own name. Fold the piece of paper in half to enclose the names. Put the folded paper on the table to the right of the candle. Place the two red roses in the vase, and put the vase on top of the folded paper.

Take the apple and, using the dressmaking pin, prick your cat's name followed by your own name into the skin. Place the apple to the right of the candle.

On the remaining small piece of paper, write your cat's name in cursive writing and join your own name to hers. Cut the pear in half and place the piece of paper bearing both names in between the two halves of the pear. Bind the two pear halves together with the pale pink or blue ribbon or thread, and place the pear in front of the candle.

Show the apple to your cat and let her see you eat it, including the core if you can. Snuff out the candle.

The following day, bury the pear in your garden or in some open space.

# AQUARIUS CAT (January 20–February 18)

*Key words: I create the magic we invent.*
*Stones or collar colours: Amethyst, Aquamarine*

Unique Aquarius familiars are sweet-natured, very spiritual, highly intelligent, and inventive in the way they bond with you. Aquarius cats are likely to tell you where their special bed or food should be placed in your home. The chances are it will be where they can see you and what you are up to.

Though genuinely loyal to you, your Aquarius familiar will at times appear to be emotionally distant. Make sure that your familiar knows where she lives so can she can find her way home. She loves everyone and everything and will like exploring outdoors. Aquarius cats may stroll into other homes around the neighbourhood and make themselves quite at home there. They may also invite neighbourhood cats into your home.

Being bright, they may find a way to unlock the cat flap or open a cupboard door. When you show attention to other people or pets, your familiar may jealously rebel and show distaste by shredding your furniture.

Aquarius cats are unlikely to pine should you go away on vacation. Instead they will form a relationship with their caregiver and other pets who are around. In your absence, they will amuse themselves and upon your return be exceptionally loving and not at all resentful.

# BONDING SPELL FOR AN
# AQUARIUS FAMILIAR

*Holly leaves, comfrey, and electric blue are all ruled by Uranus, which rules Aquarius. The folk name for the pansy is heartsease, representing love and affection between two beings. You will need:*

- Comfrey tea
- Some pansies growing in a pot
- One electric blue or silver candle
- A holly leaf or piece of paper cut into the shape of a holly leaf
- A pen with blue ink

Make yourself a cup of comfrey tea, and take it to where you are going to cast your spell.

Settle your cat close to you. Place the potted pansies beside the electric blue or silver candle, and light the candle. When the flame is established, speak your cat's name, followed by your own name, three times. Sip the comfrey tea until it is finished.

Write on the holly leaf, in cursive writing, your cat's name, followed by yours. Press the holly leaf into the soil in which the pansies are growing.

Look into the candle flame and say,

*As the candle burns*
*[Cat's name and mine]*
*Become one in*
*The light of love.*

When you feel ready, snuff out the candle.

The following day, plant the pansies on top of the holly leaf in a window box or your garden. Alternatively, keep the potted pansy indoors. In the fullness of time as the pansies grow, your relationship with your familiar will flower.

# YOUR CAT IS RULED BY EARTH IF:

Your familiar is reticent, stubborn, and a creature of habit. She is upset when you change her routine or neglect to give her attention. She is territorial and predictable and will never forsake you when you need reassurance. She is practical and materialistic, and likes you to be home with her. The Earth Signs are Taurus, Virgo, and Capricorn.

## TAURUS CAT (April 20–May 20)

*Key words: As your familiar, I possess you.*
*Stone or collar colour: Emerald*

Your Taurean familiar is loyal and comforting and able to guide you to take you out of yourself.

Taurean cats have thick necks, a solid stature, and a particularly furry tuft between their ears. Their eyes are intense and staring. Their nature is patient, affectionate, practical, and persistent. Being a creature of habit, they are upset by changes in routine. Taurean familiars may be slow to learn but will retain what they are taught.

Being fond of food, Taurean cats may bully or cajole you into overfeeding them. Taurean cats like to be the boss and will dominate other pets in the household.

Preferring the luxury of home, they will not take kindly to being put in a cattery; they think they are too special, which is true. Stubborn, Taurean cats do not like to be forced to do anything. They enjoy freedom of decision and when it is denied them, they may fly into a temper. They have robust health and generally prefer life in the countryside. They are devoted and reliable and deserving of appreciation and love, which includes sleeping on your bed and the best food you can afford.

# BONDING SPELL FOR
# A TAURUS FAMILIAR

*The pink rose, ribbon, candle, and peach—all governed by the planet
Venus, which rules Taurus—will empower your bond with your familiar.
You will need:*

- One pink candle (if your familiar is female)
- Or one blue candle (if your familiar is male)
- A peach
- A pink rose
- A pink ribbon or thread

Settle your familiar beside you and light the candle. Cut the peach in half
and remove the pit. Place the stem of the rose between the peach halves
while saying,

> *Nothing divides my familiar [name of cat] and me*
> *Only love is between us.*

Bind the two peach halves together with
the pink ribbon or thread. Stroke your cat and
sit with the candle until you feel ready to snuff
the candle out.

When you have extinguished the candle,
bury the peach and rose in your garden or an open space.

# VIRGO CAT (August 22–September 22)

*Key words: I am your truly, devoted familiar.*
*Stones or collar colours: Chrysolite, Peridot*

Beloved Virgo cats will show they love to be with you by constantly shadowing your side. They are extremely reliable critics because they know you better than you think. They are often very vocal, as well as neat and tidy and extremely clean. They are easily housebroken.

Pay attention to what they are trying to tell you because Virgo familiars are great communicators. A Virgo cat I know soiled on her owner's husband's trousers to say the husband was having an affair that she knew about before the wife did.

Virgo cats are choosy about food and unlikely to have a big appetite. They are meticulously fussy, thriving on nervous energy and in need of constant fuss and pampering. They may try to get you off the telephone or sit on your work so that you pay more attention to them. Though very sociable, they have an independent streak and on the spur of the moment may suddenly fly out of the room to have their own personal space or to be with another person or pet in your home.

Virgo familiars have a great sense of humour and for fun may suddenly pounce on you from a hiding place. Or when you are trying to sew on a button, they may run off with the cotton reel.

# BONDING SPELL FOR
# A VIRGO FAMILIAR

*Yellow and white are ruled by the planet Mercury, which governs Virgo. You will need:*

- A photograph of your cat
- A photograph of yourself
- One yellow candle
- Three white candles
- One or two paper clips

Settle your familiar close to you where she can see you cast your spell. Place the two photographs face up and side by side on your table. Put the four candles, one yellow and three white, around the photos.

Light the four candles, beginning with the yellow one. As you light each candle, speak your cat's name followed by your own name and the words,

*We are at one with each other.*

Take the two photographs and place them face to face so that your cat is looking at you and you are looking at your cat. Clip the photographs together with the paper clips.

Sit with the candles while they burn for a little while, and then snuff them out. Sleep with the photographs inside your pillowcase or keep them forever in a bedside drawer.

# CAPRICORN CAT (December 22–January 19)

*Key words: As your familiar, you are mine.*
*Stones or collar colours: Garnet, Ruby*

Capricorn familiars are very faithful. Although they are well-mannered and sociable, they are unlikely to show as much affection to others as they do to you. They are serious, even as kittens, about wanting to play with you rather than be amused by toys. You will notice that they like to climb to a high position, whether it is up trees or on top of furniture. They do not take risks or play with life. They are rather pensive cats, but have a very good sense of humour.

Loyal Capricorn cats like routine and meals fed punctually at the same time each day. They are not fussy eaters and will let little go to waste. These homebodies love to stay close by rather than wander far when let out. They retain a youthful appearance their whole life long and often have a look of sadness even though they are happy.

Capricorn cats are extraordinarily kind and considerate to children and old people. Relationships with your Capricorn familiars will be close because they will behave as if they understand every word spoken to them. They particularly need affection and praise to help them overcome an inborn shyness, sometimes seen as timidity. They are musical, so do not be surprised if their meow sounds rather like a song.

# BONDING SPELL FOR A
# CAPRICORN FAMILIAR

*In the language of flowers ivy means, "I will always cling to you." As the ivy grows, your bond with your familiar will strengthen. Both the colour brown and the ivy are ruled by the planet Saturn, which governs your familiar's birth sign. You will need:*

- One dark brown candle
- An ivy plant in a pot
- Some fur from your cat's brush

Call your familiar to your side. Place the ivy plant to the right of the brown candle. Light the candle.

Brush your familiar's fur so that she purrs. To the rhythm of your cat's purr say,

*We are bound as one and cling together in magical love.*
*Take your familiar's fur from the brush and press it into the soil in which the ivy is growing.*

# YOUR CAT IS RULED BY FIRE IF:

For no apparent reason she frenziedly flies around the room or out the door. She appears to have a playful sense of humour and tries to bring out the fun in you. Your familiar has a fiery enthusiasm for bright fires and sunshine, and a burning desire to impress people. She is dominant and willful regarding other cats or pets, as well as an independent, fearless, and avid hunter. The Fire Signs are Aries, Leo, and Sagittarius.

## ARIES CAT (March 21–April 19)

*Key words: As your familiar, I want my own way immediately.*
*Stones or collar colours: Diamond, Ruby*

Aries familiars are flirtatious with other cats and people, too. Being overly active, they demand a lot of your time and attention. They have a very big meow and often red or ginger-coloured fur. They insist on their own way and are impatient with you to give them what they want. When you disappoint them, they show their emotion by clawing furniture, your clothes, or even you. Because Aries cats are fearless, they are accident-prone as kittens and tend when older to rush into scraps with other cats.

Ruled by fire, they are attracted to flames, such as log fires, candles, and gas burners. They are adventurous and may raid your neighbours' kitchen, trash, or bird feeder for food—seizing trophies that, embarrassingly for you, they may drag through your cat flap or leave in your garden for the neighbours to see.

Being strong-willed, Aries familiars may not always come to you when called. But they are cuddly as kittens and such lovable rogues when adults that you are likely to love them for their outstanding antics.

# BONDING SPELL FOR
# AN ARIES FAMILIAR

*The planet Mars will align you and your cat's energy because it rules allspice, and the red candle and stone. You will need:*

- One red candle
- A plate
- A red stone
- Ground allspice

With your familiar close to you, place the candle in a holder on a plate. When your familiar is settled, put the red stone beside your cat so that the stone is touching her fur. Light the candle, stroke your cat, and look into the flame.

When your cat is purring or settled, sprinkle a few pinches of allspice into the candle flame and say,

*[Name of cat], I love you and you love me,*
*Bound in magic we will always be.*
*I am yours and you are mine*
*My perfect, Aries familiar feline.*

When you are ready, snuff out the candle. Keep the red stone in a spell box or bedside drawer.

# LEO CAT (July 23–August 22)

*Key words: Your familiar needs to create.*
*Stones or collar colours: Gold, Amber, Topaz*

Leo familiars love basking in the sun and are unlikely to demand to go outside when it is raining for fear of getting their magnificent fur coat wet. Leo cats often have almost mane-like neck fur and large amber eyes.

Leo cats are proud and haughty and often large and lazy. They look positively indignant when asked to move from the most comfortable seat in the house or from their spot stretched out on the floor, exactly where you need to walk. The Leo familiar rules your home and your life like a monarch. Leos like life's luxuries, such as large portions of the most expensive food. They would not think of sleeping alone, only on your bed, because they seek warmth and comfort. Ruled by the sun, your Leo cats may overdo lying in sunshine all day, resulting perhaps in sunburned ears and nose. They like attention and will seek it from you, your guests, and your neighbors too. If you have other pets, your Leo familiar will make sure she is at the top of the pecking order.

Leo cats are particularly caring parents who are very protective and attentive to their kittens, who often arrive in big litters.

# BONDING SPELL FOR A LEO FAMILIAR

*For this sun sign, use an orange or yellow candle and a bay leaf, both ruled by the sun. You can clean lipstick from your cat's paws with a cotton ball or tissue and warm water or makeup remover. You will need:*

- One orange or yellow candle
- Two pieces of white paper
- Lemon juice squeezed from a fresh lemon
- Lipstick (orange would be the most appropriate)
- A bay leaf
- A new envelope or handkerchief

Light the candle. Fill the fountain pen with lemon juice or dip the pen nib into the lemon juice to write on the first piece of paper, "My cat [name] and I are one forever." Write the date beneath.

Write your cat's name, your name, and your address in lemon juice on the second piece of white paper.

Put lipstick on your familiar's left front paw and press her paw to the front, shiny side of the bay leaf, to take your cat's left paw print. Put lipstick on your familiar's right front paw, and press it to the back of the bay leaf.

Hold the first piece of paper close enough to the candle flame to the heat, but not close enough to burn the paper. The words that you have written in lemon juice will turn brown.

Put the second piece of paper, with your cat's name and your name and address on it, along with the bay leaf in a clean envelope or handkerchief. Keep it safely in your purse where you will see it often or, alternatively, among your most intimate possessions.

Snuff out the candle. And when your familiar is ready, cuddle her or take her to bed for the night.

# SAGITTARIUS CAT (November 22–December 21)

*Key words: Daring, adventurous, humorous.*
*Stone or collar color: Turquoise*

Your Sagittarius familiar is fun, loving life and you. If ever there was a cat born with nine lives, it is the Sagittarius, born under the luck-bringing sign of Jupiter. Because the Archer is the hunter, your familiar loves chasing prey in the great outdoors, whether it is a bird, human, or another cat. They prefer the chase to the kill and have a tendency to stray or wander. They are generally sleek and lean and may incur the occasional scrape during their adventures. Active indoors, your familiar will entertain you with athletics, and although your cat may always land on her feet, objects may not land unharmed.

Your familiar is a little person. Her happy-go-lucky enthusiasm towards you will show you that she thinks you make a good team. Her intuition is strong and will tune into anything you want her to. Always in a good mood, your Sagittarius cat cannot understand why other people are not as high spirited, and she'll do what she can to try to make everyone happy.

She is not territorial and will be quite happy to share hearth and home with other pets. Your freedom-loving Sagittarius familiar is a great but independent companion who will warm your home and life with her bright, amusing presence.

# BONDING SPELL FOR A
# SAGITTARIUS FAMILIAR

*You will need:*

- Two acorns or two oak leaves
- A blue candle
- A crimson candle
- A small tin to keep the acorns in

Light both candles. Hold one acorn in your cat's left paw and the other in its right. One acorn represents you, and the other acorn represents your familiar. An acorn is symbolic of strength.

Look at the light of the candle-flame, and while holding your familiar's paws, say:

> *In spells we link through love as one*
> *May our bond be happy and good fun.*
> *I am your familiar and you are mine*
> *Our duty to each other until the end of time.*

Snuff out the candles and keep the two acorns in a tin because it and the acorns are ruled by Jupiter which rules your Sagittarius cat. As time goes by, you can add shed claws, whiskers, or milk teeth to the tin. Holding the tin and contents will establish a psychic link between you and your cat. Try telepathically calling your cat to you by holding the tin. It works.

# YOUR CAT IS RULED BY WATER IF:

Your familiar is sensitive and emotionally dependent upon you and seems to know intuitively your behaviour and actions in advance. She is secretive and also psychic, seeing things that are invisible to you. Your familiar's personality runs deep. She likes to sit by water whether it is a garden pond, a cup of tea, a shower, or a bath. She is defensive but rarely attacks. The Water Signs are Pisces, Cancer, and Scorpio.

## PISCES CAT (February 19–March 20)

*Key words: Your familiar is a dreamer.*
*Stone or collar color: Pearl*

Pisces familiars are very gentle, sensitive, and loving, and are likely to be more psychic than other felines. They are delicate in nature and easily upset. They may turn their back on you when laughed at or chastised.

They are slow to housebreak and likely to be untidy, particularly as kittens and in old age. Pisces cats will have a round face and round eyes with a faraway gaze. They will dislike solitude and enjoy the company of humans and other household pets. They are kind but liable to take a swipe when angered.

Water is a magnet to Pisces cats, who will more than likely watch you when you are washing your hair or taking a bath or shower. They may acquire the skill to drink water from the kitchen tap or bathroom, so avoid potential accidents.

If there are upheavals at home, such as painting or decorating, they will find somewhere quiet to sleep for a while. If you move, be extra careful that your Pisces familiar does not get lost, because they like to wander.

# BONDING SPELL FOR
# A PISCES FAMILIAR

*You will need:*

- One silver candle
- A dish of clean, fresh water
- A gray pebble or a shell

Settle your cat in the room in which you are going to cast your spell. Light the silver candle and place the dish of water in front of it.

Rub your cat's tail along your hand, down between the first and second fingers, then up again between the second and third fingers and down between the third and fourth finger. While you do that, say,

*I love your purr,*
*I love your soft fur.*
*In life we are one,*
*The magic has begun.*

Put the gray pebble or shell to your cat's nose for her to sniff and see. Encourage your cat to breathe life into the pebble or shell with her breath. Then drop the pebble or shell into the bowl of water.

Stroke and talk to your cat while you sit and watch the candle burn. When you feel the moment is right, snuff out the candle. Remove the pebble or shell and dry it to keep close to you or among your personal possessions. Use the water for your bath or shower, or for washing your hair.

# CANCER CAT (June 22–July 22)

*Key words: As familiars we nurture each other.*
*Stones or collar colours: Moonstone, Pearl*

Cancerian familiars are potent in their spells because they are ruled by the moon, which is visible at night when many of your spells are cast. They are the most cat-like of all cats because the moon rules the cat kingdom as a whole. Your familiar's eyes are more moon-like than any other cat's eyes. You will probably notice Cancerian cats staring into thin air, mysteriously following something with their eyes that is invisible to you, or playing with something you cannot see. These are very psychic cats. Cancerian familiars possess a sixth sense about you, your family, your home, and those dearest to you.

They love home and creature comforts. Being territorial, they are easily domesticated and quickly adapt to home and lifestyle changes, including a move. They are likely to communicate with you telepathically and understand your changing moods. Their meow is often faint and delicate, like their features.

Cancerian cats are sensitive and emotional and will be utterly devoted to you. They have crabby moods and withdraw into solitude for reasons you can never know. Telepathically, Cancerian familiars sense when you are taking them to the vet or going on vacation, even before they have seen the cat carrier or your suitcase.

Having a strong, emotional, loving attachment to you, Cancerian familiars will probably go off their food while you are away. When you return, they will not close their eyes, point their nose in the air, turn their head, and walk away from you, as if to say, "You deserted me." Instead, a warm welcome with a lot of purring awaits you.

# BONDING SPELL FOR A
# CANCERIAN FAMILIAR

*Perform this spell when the moon is full. You will need:*

- One white or silver candle
- A white lily or alternatively another
  white flower or white blossom

Light the candle. Hold your cat to your heart so that you feel or hear both your hearts beating as one. Making sure that the candle is burning safely, carry your cat to a window or into your garden where you can see the full moon.

Wait for your cat to put her front paws over your left shoulder, or place them there. Kiss her ears, nose, and two front paws and say,

*The past has gone,*
*This is today.*
*We are one forever*
*For that I pray.*

Place your cat's front paws over your right shoulder and say,

*We are one blessed by love*
*Our future is bright*
*We are linked from above*
*By eternal light day and night.*

Take your cat indoors, play together, and give your familiar lots of attention to bind the pair of you together in love. Snuff out the candle and take your cat to bed with you.

# SCORPIO CAT (October 24–November 21)

*Key words: Your familiar thinks she is the boss.*
*Stone or collar colour: Bloodstone*

Scorpio cats are secretive and more than likely of solid muscular build. They are a perfect witch's familiar because they have an uncanny ability to manipulate people as if they have bewitched them. This magical ability lies in their being highly perceptive and intuitive. If you feel that a Scorpio cat can read your mind, or put thoughts into your mind, you are right.

Scorpio familiars are passionate, purposeful, and uncompromising. If they share their home with other cats, they will want to dominate. Your complete devotion is what a Scorpio familiar will demand and enjoys most of all.

Scorpio cats do not take chances; they are sensible and not aggressive. They have a sense of humour and charisma, are genuine, predictable, and loyal. When your attention is divided, they may show signs of jealousy, disappearing in a sulk when you have company and suddenly reappearing when everyone has left. Or your familiar may stare hypnotically at your guests so that they feel uncomfortable and want to leave.

Scorpio familiars may have a hidden life, such as secretly visiting a neighbour to receive more fuss, attention, and food. When you return from a journey, they will probably turn their back on you in disgust rather than greet you.

# BONDING SPELL FOR A
# SCORPIO FAMILIAR

*Pluto governs Scorpio and your candle and spell ingredients. You will need:*

- One burgundy-coloured, dark red, or white candle
- A straight pin
- A leaf from your garden hedge, or a holly leaf or a red yew berry
- A small piece of paper (optional)
- A new envelope or handkerchief

Light the candle. With your cat lying on her back, cross your cat's paws backward and forward three times across her own chest while you look into her eyes, kiss her head, whiskers, and two front paws, and then kiss the tip of her tail while saying,

*Love is present today, to stay, always and forevermore.*
*I look into your eyes, so bright, and see the light of love.*
*I kiss your head, whiskers, ears, and front paw,*
*Our bond is a sacred kiss sealed by eternal law.*
*For our future magical tale to tell, I kiss your tail,*
*Knowing we are here for each undoubtedly without fail.*

Using a dressmaking pin, prick holes into the holly or hedge leaf to write the initials of your cat's name and yours. Draw a pinprick heart shape around the initials. Instead, you may like to press a small piece of paper, upon which you have written your initials and your cat's initials, into the red berry of a yew tree—bury the berry.

Place the leaf in a clean envelope or handkerchief and keep this in your purse so that wherever you go, your cat in thought goes with you, too. The link of love you share can never be broken by distance or time.

# CHAPTER 9

# The Cat Oracle

There are three ways to consult the Cat Oracle. When you have this book beside you and your familiar is snuggled up to you, or sitting on your lap, turn to page 103 and select a question from the list. Remember the number that is assigned to your question.

Remove the Cat Oracle board from the envelope found at the end of the book. Unfold the Cat Oracle board and place it on the floor or on a table. Spin the board around three times. With your eyes closed, randomly point to a square on the board. Open your eyes and note which of the sixteen Egyptian hieroglyphic symbols you are pointing at.

Or, if you'd like to have your familiar be more actively involved in your Oracle consultation, dangle a string across the open board and entice your cat to chase the string. As he steps on the board, note the square on which his first paw lands, and remember the Egyptian hieroglyphic symbol in that square.

Alternatively, tuck your cat firmly under one arm. With the opposite hand, gently hold one of your cat's front paws. Close your eyes and guide (not drag) his paw randomly across the board. When your hand and his paw come to a natural stop, open your eyes and note which of the Egyptian hieroglyphic symbols his paw has landed on.

# TO FIND THE ANSWER TO YOUR QUESTION

Look down the left-hand side of the Cat Oracle board and find the number of the question you chose to ask. Look at the top of the board to find the Magical symbol you or your familiar selected.

Using the your index finger on your right hand, trace a line down from the Magical symbol, and with the index finger of your left hand, trace a line across from your question number until your fingers meet on the square containing the Egyptian hieroglyphic symbol.

The page headed by the Egyptian hieroglyph is the page to consult to find your answer. Your answer appears beside the Magical symbol you or your cat randomly selected at the start of the Cat Oracle consultation.

# Questions for the Cat Oracle

1 Will the one I love, love me?

3 Will I fulfill my ambition?

5 Is my future brighter than the present?

7 Will my life become more secure?

9 Will I succeed in my new venture?

11 Will my relationship with [name of person] regain happiness?

13 Will I regain my trust in [name of person]?

15 Will I fall in love?

17 Should I forgive [name of person]?

19 What does the immediate future hold for me?

21 What does [name of person] really think of me?

23 Will the plan I have in mind succeed?

25 Is my partner faithful to me?

27 Will my finances improve?

29 How shall I know that the one I love truly loves me?

31 How will I recognize my soul mate?

| | |
|---|---|
| | Yes, because you are working hard to make it so. |
| | Rest assured that it is so. |
| | A lot more than at this moment in time. |
| | If you are cautious, yes, most definitely. |
| | You are comfortable being your own self with this person. |
| | Useful as well as lovely to know. |
| | A chance meeting with someone special. |
| | When your five senses (what you see, hear, smell, taste, and feel) agree. |
| | It is part of your destiny. |
| | Through your own actions, yes. |
| | The person will continue to love you in the same way as now. |
| | It is something that you will not regret. |
| | Eventually, yes. |
| | Yes, even slow progress is better than no progress at all. |
| | To let the person believe that you have will work greatly to your advantage. |
| | You will turn the person around with time. |

| | |
|---|---|
| | Yes, because you will find the necessary guidance and help. |
| | Reliable and trustworthy. |
| | This person is always there when needed. |
| | No, you can easily see through them and know what they are up to. |
| | You will be amazed by how much better. |
| | If you concentrate your efforts, it will be. |
| | Your minds think in the same way. |
| | They are honest and true. |
| | Something good that you have not anticipated. |
| | It is bound to. |
| | If you believe in yourself, you will fulfill your desire to succeed. |
| | Choosing good brings heavenly rewards. |
| | You are wasting your time if you think it will happen. |
| | Surprisingly, it will happen when you least expect it. |
| | It is most certainly within your power for it to happen. |
| | Undoubtedly. |

| | |
|---|---|
| | When you go on a journey, you will. |
| | It will most certainly be, if you continue to make the right choices. |
| | With a certain someone, it would be an arduous, worthless, and thankless task. |
| | What is ordained to you is wonderful, far greater than your expectations and definitely well deserved. |
| | One day it will just cross your mind and you will know that you know. |
| | Kind, warm, loving, and generous. |
| | They say that they are but are really not. |
| | A phase of hard work that brings rich rewards. |
| | This person will love you more in the future than at present. |
| | You will, but it will take time, perhaps longer than you would like. |
| | It will make the one in question feel great remorse. |
| | Not immediately, but eventually, yes. |
| | Not quickly, but steadily. |
| | You will, undoubtedly. |
| | This person will bring out the best in you. |
| | You will accomplish good results. |

| | |
|---|---|
| | Yes, if you put your mind to it. |
| | It will make you a better person. |
| | By feeling complete and fulfilled. |
| | Keep persevering and you will find that it is. |
| | An invitation to go away for a short vacation. |
| | Do not abandon it. |
| | As long as you are honest and forgiving you will. |
| | They have your best interests at heart. |
| | It will happen around a friend's birthday. |
| | Of course. |
| | You already know that this person does and will always love you. |
| | Yes, it is your destiny. |
| | Not in someone undeserving of it. |
| | It will fill your heart with happiness. |
| | A good friend who should have been treated better. |
| | These days, yes. |

| | |
|---|---|
| | You will just know it as a feeling when it happens to you. |
| | Do not doubt, because your luck is ordained in heaven. |
| | It cannot be prevented. |
| | They do not resist temptation. |
| | Without a doubt. |
| | Getting something that you have wanted for a long time. |
| | With absolute certainty. |
| | Quite unique and unobtainable. |
| | Before long, good fortune will bring you great happiness and what you seek. |
| | There are too many obstacles. |
| | Do, and you will be appreciated far more than at present. |
| | The person does and will always love you in a special way. |
| | You will, but only if you avoid distraction for a while. |
| | You are included in every possible way. |
| | Yes, you know within yourself that your mind is set upon it. |
| | You know how to endure the betrayal of artificial friends. |

| | |
|---|---|
| | No one can prevent it winning. |
| | Expect fruition soon. |
| | This person's resignation toward life amuses and strengthens you. |
| | It will never be the same again. |
| | You share an interest that is your essential nature and theirs. |
| | In the fullness of time. |
| | They are devoted. |
| | A new door is about to open into a splendid surprise. |
| | Yes, but it will take a great deal of hard work and patience, too. |
| | Many times. |
| | You will be respected and appreciated far more than at present. |
| | Yes, but not in the way that you wish it could be. |
| | The fulfillment of a love desire. |
| | It is sure to be, so try not to worry. |
| | In one person, not if you are wise. |
| | Intelligent, talented, intuitively perceptive, and enlightened. |

| | |
|---|---|
| | Whatever the circumstances, you are always warmly received. |
| | You have seen the signs, no? |
| | If you are sincere. |
| | You will feel connected. |
| | You will feel much better if you do. |
| | It is magnificent. |
| | Not in a fool. |
| | If you take positive action and avoid negative thinking. |
| | Your belief that the person will confirms your answer as yes. |
| | You will accomplish your dreams because you are in sync with good. |
| | Far too easily. |
| | You will if you have confidence in your words and deeds. |
| | It is right that it should. |
| | Strong-willed and obstinate, but very lovable. |
| | More confidence and self-esteem. |
| | Yes of course it will be, and you know it, so stay calm. |

| | |
|---|---|
| 🐸 | It would be a delusion to think so. |
| 🐈 | The damage is done. |
| 🐈 | After a lot of effort. |
| 🐈 | Too trusting of some undeserving people. |
| 🐈 | If you devote more of your time to it, yes. |
| 🐈 | Hearing from someone you used to know well. |
| 🐈 | It will remove hindrances that have blocked your personal happiness. |
| 🐈 | Yes of course. |
| 🐈 | You will have no doubt at all if you observe. |
| 🐈 | You have before and you will again. |
| 🐈 | If you dedicate yourself to it, you will. |
| 🧹 | You already know the answer is yes, so why should you not? |
| 🐈 | Your heart would have felt this person's sincere love if it were going to happen. |
| ☥ | Yes, and it will be a blessing too when it does. |
| 🐈 | Better than your expectations. |
| 🦁 | There will be no question or doubt about it when someone appears. |

| | |
|---|---|
| | It is perfectly within your capabilities to make it happen. |
| | Do, and then let go of it. |
| | The person's sincerity will shine through. |
| | Not as interested in them as they are in you. |
| | It is perfectly possible, yes. |
| | An achievement beyond your wildest dreams. |
| | In mind but not in body. |
| | They bring out the best in you and enhance your abilities. |
| | Wait and see how, most definitely, it is. |
| | Rest assured, it is. |
| | With one, most certainly not. |
| | You know better than to doubt that you will. |
| | Yes, this year. |
| | If you sincerely want, it will. |
| | You will because of your relentless efforts. |
| | You know in your heart that the person already has loving feelings for you. |

| | |
|---|---|
| | The present is not as happy as your life will be in the days, months, and years to come. |
| | Things will be unnecessarily hard if you do not. |
| | Not at the moment. |
| | You will feel that you have always known them. |
| | Better times return soon. |
| | You are protected by higher forces looking after you. |
| | Most charming, spiritually and academically gifted. |
| | They will want to show you off to their friends. |
| | You should not doubt your abilities to succeed at achieving your potential. |
| | Try harder and you will be amazed at how and when these matters unfold for you. |
| | With several wrong ones before your intended. |
| | Yes do, and continue to again and again. |
| | You will make sure that they do, that is surely true. |
| | The appreciation of respected people. |
| | This person never expected you to find out. |
| | Someone will let you know that you are loved. |

| | |
|---|---|
| ☥ | Most certainly. |
| | Someone would like to see you more often. |
| | If you work at it. |
| | Yes, for your own peace of mind as well as theirs. |
| | A reunion that you did not expect to happen. |
| | They will want to promote you and push you forward. |
| | It is the right time for it to. |
| | It is easier than you presently think it to be. |
| | With persistent patience, yes. |
| | Far more than you imagine. |
| | Certainly, and without a shadow of a doubt. |
| | You sense that the person will, and you are right. |
| | It is best that you do. |
| | It will bring you both happiness and prosperity. |
| | It is a spiritual knowing that will make itself felt. |
| | Sooner than you think. |

| | |
|---|---|
| | Someone will do a great deal for you, for love. |
| | No, because the person likes the feeling. |
| | In luck, personality, and prosperity, you are better off than the other person. |
| | Though bad now, they will be good. |
| | You share the same passion. |
| | They want it to. |
| | A better understanding with people of importance. |
| | If you do not hesitate, yes. |
| | Even though the person may be undeserving, do. |
| | In thought someone will love you, but not in genuine deed. |
| | In and out of it. |
| | If you decide to, then you will, so the choice is yours. |
| | If you try to. |
| | You have nothing to fear and a multitude of happy events awaiting you in the future. |
| | You are fortunate and will happily attain it after hardship. |
| | Quite obviously, yes, and deep inside your heart you know it will be. |

| | |
|---|---|
| | Of course it is. |
| | Only if you take more control of yourself and the situation. |
| | Today yes, but previously no. |
| | Yes, do not give up. |
| | You are easily taken advantage of. |
| | You will know it when you do. |
| | You will receive a gift and an invitation. |
| | Their actions speak louder than words. |
| | You most certainly will if you put your heart and soul into it. |
| | It will dawn on you after awhile when you are in the person's company. |
| | It is undoubtedly right. |
| | If the person were going to, you would know and feel it in your heart by now. |
| | No, not completely. |
| | Yes, a helping hand from someone who cares will make certain that it is. |
| | Yes, but a little more application to overcome hurdles is required by you. |
| | If you can find it in your heart to, yes. |

| | |
|---|---|
| | After struggles and persistence, yes. |
| | Your eyes have the same appearance. |
| | Undoubtedly. |
| | If you do, you will gain enormously. |
| | A better understanding with people you love. |
| | Yes, because if you cannot agree, you can agree to differ. |
| | Yes, and in a way that will surprise you and others who encourage you. |
| | No. You already know that they are not. |
| | You deserve someone better. |
| | You will achieve what you are aspiring to attain. |
| | You do not realize how fortunate and gifted you are. |
| | Not in the one you have in mind. |
| | You have every reason to feel optimistic. |
| | Only if you are thorough in every detail. |
| | The person's behaviour will make it evident. |
| | Next year. |

| | |
|---|---|
| | This person is honest with you. |
| | You deserve it to be, and it will be. |
| | It would be a waste of time. |
| | An easier, happier, far more sociable time than of late. |
| | If you put your mind to it, you can make them. |
| | They are easily led. |
| | You will eventually have good fortune. |
| | Fussy and unpredictable. |
| | Not as often as others will with you. |
| | It is a gift from heaven to be able to. |
| | You will be successful if you take a more positive approach. |
| | Soon, yes. |
| | You must make certain that you, or an expert you know, reads the fine print. |
| | Yes, their actions already say so. |
| | Yes, in the fullness of time. |
| | In this person's presence you are completely at ease. |

| | |
|---|---|
| | Someone puts you first. |
| | Yes, very much more. |
| | If you look elsewhere. |
| | In practical but not physical ways. |
| | Of course you will. |
| | Yes, they are. |
| | Not if you continue in one particular activity. |
| | Good news that sets you on a bright new path. |
| | You understand each other's inner sentiments. |
| | With patience, yes. |
| | With someone close to your home. |
| | Not if you have any sense. |
| | If not then, you will carry it around with you as a burden. |
| | Quirky and cute. |
| | You know that you can do it and should not delay trying. |
| | Yes, matters will work out better than you think, so have faith. |

# Index